AMERICA HURRAH

AMERICA HURRAH

by Jean-Claude van Itallie

Coward-McCann, Inc.   New York

Introduction

by Robert Brustein

Just a few days ago, a director friend was trying to convince
me that America stood on the brink of a theatrical renais-
sance that would produce at least ten dramatists of the first
rank in the next few years. At the time I found this notion
fairly preposterous but I am much more willing to entertain
it now, having just returned from Jean-Claude van Itallie's
three-play sequence, AMERICA HURRAH. I think I would
respond to Mr. van Itallie's work under any circumstances—
he speaks, if these plays are typical of him, more directly to
my own particular obsessions than any other contemporary
American playwright—but the important thing to note is that
he does not function in isolation. The workshop and cabaret
groups with which he has been associated have been collab-
orating with a surprising number of promising experimental
dramatists, and one of these groups—the Open Theatre—has
partly determined the development of his style.

The Open Theatre production of AMERICA HURRAH,
in fact, is inseparable from the plays themselves, and the dif-
ficulty of the reviewer is in finding ways to praise the playwright without helping to deliver him over to the cultural
cannibals. For if Mr. van Itallie provides the mind, spirit, and
creative impulse of the evening, the Open Theatre actors pro-
vide the technique and invention, formed over three years of

experimental work in histrionic transformation, and it would be criminal if the playwright's success led to any dissolution of this collaboration. With AMERICA HURRAH, the concept of theatrical unity finally becomes meaningful in this country and the American theatre takes three giant steps towards maturity.

The triumph of this occasion is to have found provocative theatrical images for the national malaise we have been suffering in Johnsonland these last three years: the infection of violence, calamity, indifference, gratuitous murder, and (probably the cause of all these) brutalizing war. In his first and most abstract short play, INTERVIEW, Mr. van Itallie examines, through a form of verbal and physical choreography, the mechanization of life in modern urban America. The setting is chalk white, broken by aluminum lines; four nervous job applicants from various classes of life are questioned by four bland interviewers in smiling shiny masks. The interview begins to reduce the applicants to a gaping, blinking chorus, and when they retreat into the air, the street completes the process. A young girl trying to find her way to Fourteenth Street runs a gauntlet of spastics, creeps, drunks, bizarre couples; a telephone operator is given cancer surgery with the actors transforming themselves into a failing respiratory machine; one unhappy man is given the usual ritual advice by his analyst ("Blah, blah, blah, blah, HOSTILE. Blah, blah, blah, blah, PENIS. Blah, blah, blah, blah, MOTHER. Blah, blah, blah, blah, MONEY.") while another is given customary silence by his priest; a candidate for governor dispenses hollow rhetoric on the subject of rats, red tape, four air, and Vietnam; and the play ends with the entire cast marching in place, their mouths opening and closing in a dehumanized language ("My fault" "Excuse me" "Can you help me?" "Next") from which all emotion has been evacuated. Joseph Chaikin, who founded

the Open Theatre, has directed with keen imagination, finding the exact mechanical equivalents for the automatic move-
ment of the play.

TV and MOTEL, both directed by the gifted Jacques Levy,
are more particularized works, and both make their points
through the interesting device of juxtaposition. TV, for ex-
ample, which takes place in a television rating room, juxta-
poses the eventless activities of three tired employees of the
company with melodramatic scenes from familiar television
programs (performed behind them by actors whose faces have
been made up with video lines). The effect of this is to make
a commonplace office reality act as a simple counterpoint to
the grotesqueries taking place on the screen, thus obviating
any need for satiric exaggeration (which mars most satire on
the medium). While the office workers quarrel, joke, hold a
birthday party, choke on chicken bones, etc., the television
people enact the fantasies, crimes, and aberrations of contemporary America. Wonderboy, aided by his Wondervision,
saves a housewife threatened by her monster husband; a news
program tells of the accidental killing of 60 peasants in a
friendly Vietnamese village, followed by a commercial for
cigarettes; the Lily Heaven show brings us a loudmouthed
pop singer with a Pepsodent smile, singing an endless finale
to endless applause; a Billion Dollar movie about World War
II ends with the reconciliation of two stiff lovers ("I've
learned a lot. . . . Maybe that's what war is for."); Billy
Graham addresses a crusade in Houston ("If we could look
through the ceiling of this wonderful new air-conditioned
stadium we could see the stars"), trying to reconcile great
wealth with evangelical Christianity; a situation comedy, con-
tinually interrupted by canned laughter, revolves around the
momentous question of why daughter isn't going to the prom.
By the conclusion of the play, the three employees have be-

come completely assimilated into the video action, though they haven't even been watching it, thus demonstrating, I assume, how mass culture has the power to break down our reality, whether we allow it to or not.

Mr. van Itallie's final short play is the most exciting of the evening, for it is based on a metaphor so powerful that it may well become the objective correlative of the Johnson age. Entitled MOTEL, it too is based on juxtapositions—of civilization and savagery, harmony and disorder, the nostalgic past and the terrifying present. Verbally, MOTEL is a monologue spoken by a female motelkeeper—the homey voice belongs to Ruth White, but the body is that of an enormous aproned doll with a huge carnival mask atop it, complete with hair rollers and glasses. The speech drones on about rooms ("rooms of marble and rooms of cork, all letting forth an avalanche"), rooms throughout history, and particularly this motel room with its antimacassars, hooked rugs, plastic flowers from Japan, television sets, toilets that automatically flush. As the motelkeeper proudly catalogues the room's possessions, the door opens with a blinding flash of headlights and a young couple enters—two more Artaudian mannikins on raised shoes, their huge heads bobbing, their bodies moving with the jerky menace of animated monsters. Gradually, they undress for the night, coming together for a grotesque papier mâché embrace, rubbing their cardboard bodies, then turn on the TV and, to the accompaniment of wild rock-and-roll, go about the cheerful destruction of the room: ripping off the toilet seat, breaking the bed springs, pulling down doors and windows, scrawling obscenities and pornographic drawings with lipstick on the walls, and finally tearing the motelkeeper apart, head and all. Vladimir Nabokov effectively used motel culture, in *Lolita*, as an image of the sordidness and tastelessness in the depths of our land; Mr. van Itallie uses it as an image of our violence, our insanity, our need to defile.

He has, in short, discovered the deepest poetic function of the theatre which is not, like most American dramatists, to absorb the audience into the author's own personal problems under the pretext that they are universal, but rather to invent metaphors which can poignantly suggest a nation's nightmares and afflictions. These metaphors solve nothing, change nothing, transform nothing, but they do manage to relax frustration and assuage loneliness by showing that it is still possible for men to share a common humanity—even if this only means sharing a common revulsion against what is mean and detestable. It is for this reason that I am exhilarated by these plays and by what they augur for the future of the American theatre.

AMERICA HURRAH, an evening of three short plays by Jean-Claude van Itallie, opened at the Pocket Theatre in New York City on November 7, 1966. Joseph Chaikin directed the first play, INTERVIEW. Jacques Levy directed TV and MOTEL. The producer was Stephanie Sills. Costumes: Tania Leontov. Stage Manager and Lighting Designer: Ken Glickfeld.

Illustrations will be found at page 72

INTERVIEW

A Fugue for Eight Actors

INTERVIEW was first performed in 1965 (in an earlier version
and under the title PAVANE) at the Academy Theatre in At-
lanta. An Open Theatre production was directed at about the
same time by Peter Feldman; it was presented for one night
at the Sheridan Square Playhouse and then at the Cafe La
Mama. The La Mama Troupe performed the play in Europe
under the direction of Tom O'Horgan, who also directed the
play for National Educational TV. INTERVIEW would not exist
in its present form, however, without the collaboration, in
rehearsal, of Joseph Chaikin and the actors in AMERICA
HURRAH. The cast:

First Interviewer	Cynthia Harris
First Applicant	Conard Fowkes
Second Applicant	Ronnie Gilbert
Third Applicant	Henry Calvert
Fourth Applicant	Joyce Aaron
Second Interviewer	James Barbosa
Third Interviewer	Brenda Smiley
Fourth Interviewer	Bill Macy

The set is white and impersonal.

4 women
4 men

Two subway stairs are at the back of the stage. On the sides there is one entrance for Applicants and another entrance for Interviewers.

The only furniture or props needed are eight grey blocks.

The actors, four men and four women, are dressed in black-and-white street clothes. During the employment agency section only, Interviewers wear translucent plastic masks.

There is an intermittent harpsichord accompaniment: dance variations (minuet, Virginia reel, twist) on a familiar American tune. But much of the music (singing, whistling, humming) is provided by the actors on stage. It is suggested, moreover, that as a company of actors and a director approach the play they find their own variations in rhythmic expression. The successful transition from one setting to the next depends on the actors' ability to play together as a company and to drop character instantaneously and completely in order to assume another character, or for a group effect.

(*The First Interviewer for an employment agency, a young woman, sits on stage as the First Applicant, a Housepainter, enters.*)

FIRST INTERVIEWER (*standing*). How do you do?

FIRST APPLICANT (*sitting*). Thank you, I said, not knowing where to sit.

(*The characters will often include the audience in what they say, as if they were being interviewed by the audience.*)

FIRST INTERVIEWER (*pointedly*). Won't you sit down?

FIRST APPLICANT (*standing again quickly, afraid to displease*).
I'm sorry.

FIRST INTERVIEWER (*busy with imaginary papers, pointing to a particular seat*). There. Name, please?

FIRST APPLICANT. Jack Smith.

FIRST INTERVIEWER. Jack what Smith?

FIRST APPLICANT. Beg pardon?

FIRST INTERVIEWER. Fill in the blank space, please. Jack blank space Smith.

FIRST APPLICANT. I don't have any.

FIRST INTERVIEWER. I asked you to sit down.
    (*pointing*)
There.

FIRST APPLICANT (*sitting*). I'm sorry.

FIRST INTERVIEWER. Name, please?

FIRST APPLICANT. Jack Smith.

FIRST INTERVIEWER. You haven't told me your MIDDLE name.

FIRST APPLICANT. I haven't got one.

FIRST INTERVIEWER (*suspicious but writing it down*). No middle name.

(*Second Applicant, a woman, a Floorwasher, enters.*)

FIRST INTERVIEWER. How do you do?

SECOND APPLICANT (*sitting*). Thank you, I said, not knowing what.

FIRST INTERVIEWER. Won't you sit down?

SECOND APPLICANT (*standing*). I'm sorry.

FIRST APPLICANT. I am sitting.

FIRST INTERVIEWER (*pointing*). There. Name, please?

SECOND APPLICANT (*sitting*). Jane Smith.

FIRST APPLICANT. Jack Smith.

FIRST INTERVIEWER. What blank space Smith?

SECOND APPLICANT. Ellen.

FIRST APPLICANT. Haven't got one.

FIRST INTERVIEWER. What job are you applying for?

FIRST APPLICANT. Housepainter.

SECOND APPLICANT. Floorwasher.

FIRST INTERVIEWER. We haven't many vacancies in that. What experience have you had?

FIRST APPLICANT. A lot.

SECOND APPLICANT. Who needs experience for floorwashing?

FIRST INTERVIEWER. You will help me by making your answers clear.

FIRST APPLICANT. Eight years.

SECOND APPLICANT. Twenty years.

(*Third Applicant, a Banker, enters.*)

FIRST INTERVIEWER. How do you do?

SECOND APPLICANT. I'm good at it.

FIRST APPLICANT. Very well.

THIRD APPLICANT (*sitting*). Thank you, I said, as casually as I could.

FIRST INTERVIEWER. Won't you sit down?

THIRD APPLICANT (*standing again*). I'm sorry.

SECOND APPLICANT. I am sitting.

FIRST APPLICANT (*standing again*). I'm sorry.

FIRST INTERVIEWER (*pointing to a particular seat*).   There. Name, please?

FIRST APPLICANT.   Jack Smith.

SECOND APPLICANT.   Jane Smith.

THIRD APPLICANT.   Richard Smith.

FIRST INTERVIEWER.   What EXACTLY Smith, please?

THIRD APPLICANT.   Richard F.

SECOND APPLICANT.   Jane Ellen.

FIRST APPLICANT.   Jack None.

FIRST INTERVIEWER.   What are you applying for?

FIRST APPLICANT.   Housepainter.

SECOND APPLICANT.   I need money.

THIRD APPLICANT.   Bank president.

FIRST INTERVIEWER.   How many years have you been in your present job?

THIRD APPLICANT.   Three.

SECOND APPLICANT.   Twenty.

FIRST APPLICANT.   Eight.

(*Fourth Applicant, a Lady's Maid, enters.*)

FIRST INTERVIEWER.   How do you do?

FOURTH APPLICANT.   I said thank you, not knowing where to sit.

THIRD APPLICANT.   I'm fine.

SECOND APPLICANT.   Do I have to tell you?

FIRST APPLICANT.   Very well.

FIRST INTERVIEWER.   Won't you sit down?

FOURTH APPLICANT.   I'm sorry.

THIRD APPLICANT (*sitting again*).   Thank you.

SECOND APPLICANT (*standing again*).   I'm sorry.

FIRST APPLICANT (*sitting*).   Thanks.

FIRST INTERVIEWER (*pointing to a particular seat*).   There. Name, please?

(*Fourth Applicant sits.*)

ALL APPLICANTS.   Smith.

FIRST INTERVIEWER.   What Smith?

FOURTH APPLICANT.   Mary Victoria.

THIRD APPLICANT.   Richard F.

SECOND APPLICANT.   Jane Ellen.

FIRST APPLICANT.   Jack None.

FIRST INTERVIEWER.   How many years' experience have you had?

FOURTH APPLICANT.   Eight years.

SECOND APPLICANT.   Twenty years.

FIRST APPLICANT.   Eight years.

THIRD APPLICANT.   Three years four months and nine days not counting vacations and sick leave and the time both my daughters and my wife had the whooping cough.

FIRST INTERVIEWER.   Just answer the questions, please.

FOURTH APPLICANT.   Yes, sir.

THIRD APPLICANT.   Sure.

SECOND APPLICANT.   I'm sorry.

FIRST APPLICANT.   That's what I'm doing.

(Second Interviewer, a young man, enters and goes to inspect Applicants. With the entrance of each Interviewer, the speed of the action accelerates.)

SECOND INTERVIEWER. How do you do?

FIRST APPLICANT (*standing*). I'm sorry.

SECOND APPLICANT (*sitting*). Thank you.

THIRD APPLICANT (*standing*). I'm sorry.

FOURTH APPLICANT (*sitting*). Thank you.

SECOND INTERVIEWER. What's your name?

FIRST INTERVIEWER. Your middle name, please.

FIRST APPLICANT. Smith.

SECOND APPLICANT. Ellen.

THIRD APPLICANT. Smith, Richard F.

FOURTH APPLICANT. Mary Victoria Smith.

FIRST INTERVIEWER. What is your exact age?

SECOND INTERVIEWER. Have you any children?

FIRST APPLICANT. I'm thirty-two years old.

SECOND APPLICANT. One son.

THIRD APPLICANT. I have two daughters.

FOURTH APPLICANT. Do I have to tell you that?

FIRST INTERVIEWER.   Are you married, single, or other?

SECOND INTERVIEWER.   Have you ever earned more than that?

FIRST APPLICANT.   No.

SECOND APPLICANT.   Never.

THIRD APPLICANT.   Married.

FOURTH APPLICANT.   Single, NOW.

(*Third Interviewer, a woman, enters.*)

THIRD INTERVIEWER.   How do you do?

FIRST APPLICANT (*sitting*).   Thank you.

SECOND APPLICANT (*standing*).   I'm sorry.

THIRD APPLICANT (*sitting*).   Thank you.

FOURTH APPLICANT (*standing*).   I'm sorry.

(*Fourth Interviewer, a man, appears on the heels of Third Interviewer.*)

FOURTH INTERVIEWER.   How do you do?

FIRST APPLICANT (*standing*).   I'm sorry.

SECOND APPLICANT (*sitting*).   Thank you.

THIRD APPLICANT (*standing*). I'm sorry.

FOURTH APPLICANT (*sitting*). Thank you.

ALL INTERVIEWERS. What is your Social Security Number, please?

(*Applicants do the next four speeches simultaneously.*)

FIRST APPLICANT. 333 dash 6598 dash 5590765439 dash 003.

SECOND APPLICANT. 999 dash 5733 dash 699075432 dash 11.

THIRD APPLICANT (*sitting*). I'm sorry. I left it home. I can call if you let me use the phone.

FOURTH APPLICANT. I always get it confused with my Checking Account Number.

(*Interviewers do the next four speeches in a round.*)

FIRST INTERVIEWER. Will you be so kind as to tell me a little about yourself?

SECOND INTERVIEWER. Can you fill me in on something about your background please?

THIRD INTERVIEWER. It'd be a help to our employers if you'd give me a little for our files.

FOURTH INTERVIEWER. Now what would you say, say, to a prospective employer about yourself?

(*Applicants address parts of the following four speeches, in particular, directly to the audience.*)

FIRST APPLICANT. I've been a Union member twenty years, I said to them, if that's the kind of thing you want to know. Good health, I said. Veteran of two wars. Three kids. Wife's dead. Wife's sister, she takes care of them. I don't know why I'm telling you this, I said smiling.
(*sits*)

SECOND APPLICANT (*standing*). So what do you want to know, I told the guy. I've been washin' floors for twenty years. Nobody's ever complained. I don't loiter after hours, I said to him. Just because my boy's been in trouble is no reason, I said, no reason—I go right home, I said to him. Right home.
(*sits*)

THIRD APPLICANT (*standing*). I said that I was a Republican and we could start right there. And then I said that I spend most of my free time watching television or playing in the garden of my four-bedroom house with our two lovely daughters, aged nine and eleven. I mentioned that my wife plays with us too, and that her name is Katherine, although, I said casually, her good friends call her Kitty. I wasn't at all nervous.
(*sits*)

FOURTH APPLICANT (*standing*). Just because I'm here, sir, I told him, is no reason for you to patronize me. I've been a lady's maid, I said, in houses you would not be allowed into. My father was a gentleman of leisure, AND what's more, I said, my references are unimpeachable.

FIRST INTERVIEWER. I see.

SECOND INTERVIEWER. All right.

THIRD INTERVIEWER. That's fine.

FOURTH INTERVIEWER. Of course.

(*Applicants do the following four speeches simultaneously.*)

FIRST APPLICANT. Just you call anybody at the Union and ask them. They'll hand me a clean bill of health.

SECOND APPLICANT. I haven't been to jail if that's what you mean. Not me. I'm clean.

THIRD APPLICANT. My record is impeccable. There's not a stain on it.

FOURTH APPLICANT. My references would permit me to be a governess, that's what.

FIRST INTERVIEWER (*going to First Applicant and inspecting under his arms*). When did you last have a job house-painting?

SECOND INTERVIEWER (*going to Second Applicant and inspecting her teeth*). Where was the last place you worked?

THIRD INTERVIEWER (*going to Third Applicant and inspecting him*). What was your last position in a bank?

FOURTH INTERVIEWER (*going to Fourth Applicant and inspecting her*). Have you got your references with you?

(*Applicants do the following four speeches simultaneously, with music under.*)

FIRST APPLICANT. I've already told you I worked right along till I quit.

SECOND APPLICANT. Howard Johnson's on Fifty-first Street all last month.

THIRD APPLICANT. First Greenfield International and Franklin Banking Corporation Banking and Stone Incorporated.

FOURTH APPLICANT. I've got a letter right here in my bag. Mrs. Muggintwat only let me go because she died.

(*Interviewers do the next four speeches in a round.*)

FIRST INTERVIEWER (*stepping around and speaking to Second Applicant*). Nothing terminated your job at Howard Johnson's? No franks, say, missing at the end of the day, I suppose?

SECOND INTERVIEWER (*stepping around and speaking to Third Applicant*). It goes without saying, I suppose, that you could stand an FBI Security Test?

THIRD INTERVIEWER (*stepping around and speaking to Fourth Applicant*). I suppose there are no records of minor thefts or, shall we say, borrowings from your late employer?

FOURTH INTERVIEWER (*stepping around and speaking to First Applicant*). Nothing political in your Union dealings? Nothing Leftist, I suppose? Nothing Rightist either, I hope.

(*Applicants and Interviewers line up for a square dance. Music under the following.*)

FIRST APPLICANT (*bowing to First Interviewer*). What's it to you, buddy?

SECOND APPLICANT (*bowing to Second Interviewer*). Eleanor Roosevelt wasn't more honest.

THIRD APPLICANT (*bowing to Third Interviewer*). My record is lily-white, sir!

FOURTH APPLICANT (*bowing to Fourth Interviewer*). Mrs. Thumbletwat used to take me to the bank and I'd watch her open her box!

(*Each Interviewer, during his next speech, goes upstage to form another line.*)

FIRST INTERVIEWER. Good!

SECOND INTERVIEWER. Fine!

THIRD INTERVIEWER. Swell!

FOURTH INTERVIEWER. Fine!

(*Applicants come downstage together; they do the next four speeches simultaneously and directly to the audience.*)

FIRST APPLICANT.   I know my rights. As a veteran. AND a citizen. I know my rights. AND my cousin is very well-known in certain circles, if you get what I mean. In the back room of a certain candy store in the Italian district of this city my cousin is VERY well known, if you get what I mean. I know my rights. And I know my cousin.

SECOND APPLICANT (*putting on a pious act, looking up to heaven*).   Holy Mary Mother of God, must I endure all the sinners of this earth? Must I go on a poor washerwoman in this City of Sin? Help me, oh my God, to leave this earthly crust, and damn your silly impudence, young man, if you think you can treat an old woman like this. You've got another thought coming, you have.

THIRD APPLICANT.   I have an excellent notion to report you to the Junior Chamber of Commerce of this city of which I am the Secretary and was in line to be elected Vice President and still will be if you are able to find me gainful and respectable employ!

FOURTH APPLICANT.   Miss Thumblebottom married into the Twiths and if you start insulting me, young man, you'll have to start in insulting the Twiths as well. A Twith isn't a nobody, you know, as good as a Thumbletwat, AND they all call me their loving Mary, you know.

ALL INTERVIEWERS (*in a loud raucous voice*).   Do you smoke?

(*Each Applicant, during his next speech, turns upstage.*)

FIRST APPLICANT.   No thanks.

SECOND APPLICANT.   Not now.

THIRD APPLICANT.   No thanks.

FOURTH APPLICANT.   Not now.

ALL INTERVIEWERS (*again in a harsh voice and bowing or curtsying*).   Do you mind if I do?

FIRST APPLICANT.   I don't care.

SECOND APPLICANT.   Who cares?

THIRD APPLICANT.   Course not.

FOURTH APPLICANT.   Go ahead.

(*Interviewers form a little group off to themselves.*)

FIRST INTERVIEWER.   I tried to quit but couldn't manage.

SECOND INTERVIEWER.   I'm a three-pack-a-day man, I guess.

THIRD INTERVIEWER.   If I'm gonna go I'd rather go smoking.

FOURTH INTERVIEWER.   I'm down to five a day.

(*Applicants all start to sneeze.*)

FIRST APPLICANT.   Excuse me, I'm gonna sneeze.

SECOND APPLICANT.   Have you got a hanky?

THIRD APPLICANT.   I have a cold coming on.

FOURTH APPLICANT.   I thought I had some tissues in my bag.

(*Applicants all sneeze.*)

FIRST INTERVIEWER.   Gezundheit.

SECOND INTERVIEWER.   God bless you.

THIRD INTERVIEWER.   Gezundheit.

FOURTH INTERVIEWER.   God bless you.

(*Applicants all sneeze simultaneously.*)

FIRST INTERVIEWER.   God bless you.

SECOND INTERVIEWER.   Gezundheit.

THIRD INTERVIEWER.   God bless you.

FOURTH INTERVIEWER.   Gezundheit.

(*Applicants return to their seats.*)

FIRST APPLICANT.   Thanks, I said.

SECOND APPLICANT.   I said thanks.

THIRD APPLICANT.   Thank you, I said.

FOURTH APPLICANT.   I said thank you.

(*Interviewers stand on their seats and say the following as if one person were speaking.*)

FIRST INTERVIEWER.   Do you

SECOND INTERVIEWER.   speak any

THIRD INTERVIEWER.   foreign

FOURTH INTERVIEWER.   languages?

FIRST INTERVIEWER.   Have you

SECOND INTERVIEWER.   got a

THIRD INTERVIEWER.   college

FOURTH INTERVIEWER.   education?

FIRST INTERVIEWER.   Do you

SECOND INTERVIEWER.   take

THIRD INTERVIEWER.   shorthand?

FOURTH INTERVIEWER.   Have you

FIRST INTERVIEWER.   any

SECOND INTERVIEWER.   special

THIRD INTERVIEWER.   qualifications?

FIRST INTERVIEWER.   Yes?

FIRST APPLICANT (*stepping up to Interviewers*).   Sure, I can
speak Italian, I said. My whole family is Italian so I oughta

be able to, and I can match colors, like green to green, so that even your own mother couldn't tell the difference, begging your pardon, I said, I went through the eighth grade.

(*steps back*)

SECOND INTERVIEWER.   Next.

SECOND APPLICANT (*stepping up to Interviewers*).   My grand-mother taught me some Gaelic, I told the guy. And my old man could rattle off in Yiddish when he had a load on. I never went to school at all excepting church school, but I can write my name good and clear. Also, I said, I can smell an Irishman or a Yid a hundred miles off.

(*steps back*)

THIRD INTERVIEWER.   Next.

THIRD APPLICANT (*stepping up to Interviewers*).   I've never had any need to take shorthand in my position, I said to him. I've a Z.A. in business administration from Philadel-phia, and a Z.Z.A. from M.Y.U. night school. I mentioned that I speak a little Spanish, of course, and that I'm a whiz at model frigates and warships.

(*steps back*)

FOURTH INTERVIEWER.   Next.

FOURTH APPLICANT (*stepping up to Interviewers*).   I can sew a straight seam, I said, hand or machine, and I have been exclusively a lady's maid although I CAN cook and will too if I have someone to assist me, I said. Unfortunately, aside from self-education, grammar school is as far as I have progressed.

(*steps back*)

(*Each Interviewer, during his next speech, bows or curtsies to the Applicant nearest him.*)

FIRST INTERVIEWER. Good.

SECOND INTERVIEWER. Fine.

THIRD INTERVIEWER. Very helpful.

FOURTH INTERVIEWER. Thank you.

(*Each Applicant, during his next speech, jumps on the back of the Interviewer nearest him.*)

FOURTH APPLICANT. You're welcome, I'm sure.

THIRD APPLICANT. Anything you want to know.

SECOND APPLICANT. Just ask me.

FIRST APPLICANT. Fire away, fire away.

(*The next eight speeches are spoken simultaneously, with Applicants on Interviewers' backs.*)

FIRST INTERVIEWER. //Well unless there's anything special you want to tell me, I think—

SECOND INTERVIEWER. Is there anything more you think I should know about before you—

THIRD INTERVIEWER.   I wonder if we've left anything out of this questionnaire or if you—

FOURTH INTERVIEWER.   I suppose I've got all the information down here unless you can—

FIRST APPLICANT.   I've got kids to support, you know, and I need a job real quick—

SECOND APPLICANT.   Do you think you could try and get me something today because I—

THIRD APPLICANT.   How soon do you suppose I can expect to hear from your agency? Do you—

FOURTH APPLICANT.   I don't like to sound pressureful, but you know I'm currently on unemploy—

(*Each Applicant, during his next speech, jumps off Interviewer's back.*)

FIRST APPLICANT.   Beggin' your pardon.

SECOND APPLICANT.   So sorry.

THIRD APPLICANT.   Excuse me.

FOURTH APPLICANT.   Go ahead.

(*Each Interviewer, during his next speech, bows or curtsies and remains in that position.*)

FIRST INTERVIEWER.   That's quite all right.

SECOND INTERVIEWER. I'm sorry.

THIRD INTERVIEWER. I'm sorry.

FOURTH INTERVIEWER. My fault.

(*Each Applicant, during his next speech, begins leap-frogging over Interviewers' backs.*)

FIRST APPLICANT. My fault.

SECOND APPLICANT. My fault.

THIRD APPLICANT. I'm sorry.

FOURTH APPLICANT. My fault.

(*Each Interviewer, during his next speech, begins leap-frogging too.*)

FIRST INTERVIEWER. That's all right.

SECOND INTERVIEWER. My fault.

THIRD INTERVIEWER. I'm sorry.

FOURTH INTERVIEWER. Excuse me.

(*The leap-frogging continues as the preceding eight lines are repeated simultaneously. Then the Interviewers confer in a huddle and come out of it.*)

FIRST INTERVIEWER. Do you enjoy your work?

FIRST APPLICANT.   Sure, I said, I'm proud. Why not? Sure I know I'm no Rembrandt, I said, but I'm proud of my work, I said to him.

SECOND APPLICANT.   I told him it stinks. But what am I supposed to do, sit home and rot?

THIRD APPLICANT.   Do I like my work, he asked me. Well, I said, to gain time, do I like my work? Well, I said, I don't know.

FOURTH APPLICANT.   I told him right straight out: for a sensible person, a lady's maid is the ONLY POSSIBLE way of life.

SECOND INTERVIEWER.   Do you think you're irreplaceable?

ALL APPLICANTS.   Oh, yes indeed.

ALL INTERVIEWERS.   Irreplaceable?

ALL APPLICANTS.   Yes, yes indeed.

THIRD INTERVIEWER.   Do you like me?

FIRST APPLICANT.   You're a nice man.

SECOND APPLICANT.   Huh?

THIRD APPLICANT.   Why do you ask?

FOURTH APPLICANT.   It's not a question of LIKE.

FIRST INTERVIEWER.   Well, we'll be in touch with you.

(This is the beginning of leaving the agency. Soft music under. Applicants and Interviewers push their seats into two masses of four boxes, one on each side of the stage. Applicants leave first, joining hands to form a revolving door.

All are now leaving the agency, not in any orderly fashion. Interviewers start down one of the subway stairs at the back of the stage and Applicants start down the other. The following speeches overlap and are heard indistinctly as crowd noise.)

FOURTH INTERVIEWER.   What sort of day will it be?

FIRST APPLICANT.   I bet we'll have rain.

SECOND APPLICANT.   Cloudy, clearing in the afternoon.

THIRD APPLICANT.   Mild, I think, with some snow.

FOURTH APPLICANT.   Precisely the same as yesterday.

SECOND APPLICANT.   Can you get me one?

FIRST INTERVIEWER.   See you tomorrow.

THIRD APPLICANT.   When will I hear from you?

SECOND INTERVIEWER.   We'll let you know.

FOURTH APPLICANT.   Where's my umbrella?

THIRD INTERVIEWER.   I'm going to a movie.

FIRST APPLICANT.   So how about it?

FOURTH INTERVIEWER.   Good night.

THIRD APPLICANT.   Can you help me, Doctor, I asked.

(*When all of the actors are offstage, the Fourth Interviewer makes a siren sound and the following speeches continue from downstairs as a loud crowd noise for a few moments; they overlap so that the stage is empty only briefly.*)

FIRST INTERVIEWER.   It'll take a lot of work on your part.

SECOND INTERVIEWER.   I'll do what I can for you.

THIRD INTERVIEWER.   Of course I'll do my best.

FIRST INTERVIEWER.   God helps those who help themselves.

FIRST APPLICANT.   I have sinned deeply, Father, I said.

FIRST INTERVIEWER.   You certainly have. I hope you truly repent.

SECOND INTERVIEWER.   In the name of the Father, etcetera, and the Holy Ghost.

THIRD INTERVIEWER.   Jesus saves.

FOURTH APPLICANT.   I said can you direct me to Fourteenth Street, please?

FIRST INTERVIEWER.   Just walk down that way a bit and then turn left.

SECOND INTERVIEWER. Just walk down that way a bit and then turn right.

THIRD INTERVIEWER. Take a cab!

FOURTH APPLICANT. Do you hear a siren?

ALL INTERVIEWERS. What time is it?

FIRST APPLICANT. Half-past three.

SECOND APPLICANT. It must be about four.

THIRD APPLICANT. Half-past five.

FOURTH APPLICANT. My watch has stopped.

FIRST INTERVIEWER. Do you enjoy your work?

SECOND INTERVIEWER. Do you think you're irreplaceable?

THIRD INTERVIEWER. Do you like me?

(*The actor who played the Fourth Interviewer comes on stage while continuing to make the loud siren noise. The actress who played the Fourth Applicant comes on stage and speaks directly to the audience.*)

FOURTH APPLICANT. Can you direct me to Fourteenth Street, please, I said. I seem to have lost my—I started to say, and then I was nearly run down.

(*The remaining actors return to the stage to play various people on Fourteenth Street: ladies shopping, a panhan-*

dler, a man in a sandwich board, a peddler of "franks and orange," a snooty German couple, a lecher, a pair of sighing lovers, and so on. The actors walk straight forward toward the audience and then walk backwards to the rear of the stage. Each time they approach the audience, they do so as a different character. The actor will need to find the essential vocal and physical manner- isms of each character, play them, and drop them imme- diately to assume another character. The Fourth Appli- cant continues to address the audience directly, to in- volve them in her hysteria, going up the aisle and back.)

FOURTH APPLICANT. I haven't got my Social Security—I started to say, I saw someone right in front of me and I said, could you direct me please to Fourteenth Street, I have to get to Fourteenth Street, please, to get a bargain, I ex- plained, although I could hardly remember what it was I wanted to buy. I read about it in the paper today, I said, only they weren't listening and I said to myself, my pur- pose for today is to get to—and I couldn't remember, I've set myself the task of—I've got to have—it's that I can save, I remembered, I can save if I can get that bargain at—and I couldn't remember where it was so I started to look for my wallet which I seem to have mislaid in my purse, and a man—please watch where you're going, I shouted with my purse half-open, and I seemed to forget—Fourteenth Street, I remembered, and you'd think with all these num- bered streets and avenues a person wouldn't get lost—you'd think a person would HELP a person, you'd think so. So I asked the most respectable looking man I could find, I asked him, please can you direct me to Fourteenth Street. He wouldn't answer. Just wouldn't. I'm lost, I said to my- self. The paper said—the television said—they said, I couldn't remember what they said. I turned for help: "Jesus Saves" the sign said, and a man was carrying it, both sides of his body, staring straight ahead. "Jesus Saves" the sign said.

(*The passers-by jostle her more and more.*)

FOURTH APPLICANT.   I couldn't remember where I was going. "Come and be saved" it said, so I asked the man with the sign, please, sir, won't you tell me how to, dear Lord, I thought, anywhere, please, sir, won't you tell me how to— can you direct me to Fourteenth Street, PLEASE!

(*The passers-by have covered the Fourth Applicant. All actors mill about until they reach designated positions on the stage where they face the audience, a line of women and a line of men, students in a gym class. The Second Interviewer has stayed coolly out of the crowd during this last; now he is the Gym Instructor.*)

GYM INSTRUCTOR.   I took my last puff and strode resolutely into the room. Ready men, I asked brightly. And one and two and three and four and one and two and keep it up.

(*The Gym Instructor is trying to help his students mold themselves into the kind of people seen in advertisements and the movies. As he counts to four the students puff out their chests, smile, and look perfectly charming. As he counts to four again, the students relax and look ordinary.*)

GYM INSTRUCTOR.   You wanna look like the guys in the movies, don't you, I said to the fellahs. Keep it up then. You

wanna radiate that kinda charm and confidence they have
in the movies, don't you, I said to the girls. Keep it up
then, stick 'em out, that's what you got 'em for. Don't be
ashamed. All of you, tuck in your butts, I said loudly.
That's the ticket, I said, wishing to hell I had a cigarette.
You're selling, selling all the time, that right, miss? Keep
on selling, I said. And one and two and three and four and
ever see that guy on TV, I said. What's his name, I asked
them. What's his name? Aw, you know his name, I said,
forgetting his name. Never mind, it'll come to you, I said.
He comes in here too. See that, I said, grabbing a guy out
of line and showing 'em his muscle. See that line, I said,
making the guy feel good, know what that is? It's boyish-
ness, I said. You come here, I said, throwing him back into
the line, and it'll renew your youthfulness, I said, taking a
deep breath. And one and two and three and four and
smile, I said, smiling. Not so big, I said, smiling less. You
look like creeps, I said, when you smile that big. When you
smile, hold something back. Make like you're holding back
something big, I said, a secret, I said. That's the ticket.
And one and two and three and four and . . .
    (*accelerating the rhythm to a double count*)
Anybody got a cigarette, I said suddenly, without thinking.
I was just kidding, I said then, sheepishly. One and two
and three and four, I said, wishing I had a cigarette. And
one and two and three and four . . .

    (*The rapid movements of the gym class become the vi-
brations of passengers on a moving subway train. The
actors rush to the boxes stage left, continuing to vibrate.
Two of the actors stand on the boxes and smile like subway advertisements while the others, directly in front of
them, are pushed against each other on the crowded*

*train. They make an appropriate soft subway noise, a
kind of rhythmic hiss and, as the subway passengers, form
their faces into frozen masks of indifference.*)

SECOND APPLICANT (*squeezing her way to an uncomfortable
front seat and speaking half to herself*). God forgive me
. . . you no-good chump, I said to him, I used to love
you . . . not now. Not now . . . God forgive me . . .
God forgive me for being old. Not now, I said. I wouldn't
wipe the smell off your uncle's bottom now, not for turnips,
no. God forgive me . . . Remember how we used to ride
the roller coaster out at Coney Island, you and me? Remember? Holding hands in the cold and I'd get so scared
and you'd get so scared and we'd hug each other and buy
another ticket . . . Remember? . . . Look now, I said.
Look at me now! God forgive you for leaving me with
nothing . . . God forgive you for being dead . . . God
forgive me for being alive . . .

(*The actress who played the Third Interviewer slips out
of the subway as though it were her stop and sits on a
box, stage right, as a Telephone Operator. The other
actors form a telephone circuit by holding hands in two
concentric circles around the boxes, stage left; they
change the hissing sound of the subway into the whistling
of telephone circuits.*)

TELEPHONE OPERATOR.   Just one moment and I will connect
you with Information.

(*The Telephone Operator alternates her official voice
with her ordinary voice; she uses the latter when she
talks to her friend Roberta, another operator whom she*

*reaches by flipping a switch. When she is talking to
Roberta, the whistling of the telephone circuit changes
into a different rhythm and the arms of the actors, which
are forming the circuit, move into a different position.)*

TELEPHONE OPERATOR.   Just one moment and I will connect
you with Information. Ow! Listen, Roberta, I said, I've
got this terrible cramp. Hang up and dial again, please; we
find nothing wrong with that number at all. You know
what I ate, I said to her, you were there. Baked macaroni,
Wednesday special, maple-nut fudge, I said. I'm sorry but
the number you have reached is not—I can feel it gnawing
at me at the bottom of my belly, I told her. Do you think
it's serious, Roberta? Appendicitis? I asked. Thank you for
giving us the area code but the number you have reached
is not in this area. Roberta, I asked her, do you think I have
cancer? One moment, please, I'm sorry the number you
have reached—ow! Well, if it's lunch, Roberta, I said to
her, you know what they can do with it tomorrow. Ow!
One moment, please, I said. Ow, I said, Roberta, I said, it
really hurts.

*(The Telephone Operator falls off her seat in pain. The
whistling of the telephone circuit becomes a siren. Three
actors carry the Telephone Operator over to the boxes,
stage left, which now serve as an operating table. Three
actors imitate the Telephone Operator's breathing pattern while four actors behind her make stylized sounds
and movements as surgeons and nurses in the midst of
an operation. The Telephone Operator's breathing accelerates, then stops. After a moment the actors begin
spreading over the stage and making the muted sounds
of a cocktail party: music, laughter, talk. The actors find*

a position and remain there, playing various aspects of a
party in slow motion and muted tones. They completely
ignore the First Interviewer who, as a Girl At The Party,
goes from person to person as if she were in a garden of
living statues.)

GIRL AT THE PARTY (*rapidly and excitedly*). And then after
the ambulance took off I went up in the elevator and into
the party. Did you see the accident, I asked, and they said
they did, and what did he look like, and I said he wore a
brown coat and had straight brown hair. He stepped off
the curb right in front of me. We had been walking up
the same block, he a few feet ahead of me, this block right
here, I said, but she wasn't listening. Hi, my name is Jill,
I said to somebody sitting down and they looked at me and
smiled so I said his arm was torn out of its socket and his
face was on the pavement gasping but I didn't touch him
and she smiled and walked away and I said after her, you
aren't supposed to touch someone before—I WANTED to
help, I said, but she wasn't listening. When a man came
up and said was it someone you knew and I said yes, it
was someone I knew slightly, someone I knew, yes, and
he offered me a drink and I said no thanks, I didn't want
one, and he said well how well did I know him, and I said
I knew him well, yes, I knew him very well. You were
coming together to the party, he said. Yes, I said, excuse
me. Hi, my name is Jill, did you hear a siren, and they said
oh you're the one who saw it, was he killed?

(*becoming resigned to the fact that no one is listening*)
And I said yes I was, excuse me, and went back across the
room but couldn't find another face to talk to until I deliberately bumped into somebody because I had to tell
them one of us couldn't come because of the accident. It

was Jill. Jill couldn't come. I'm awfully sorry, I said, because of the accident. She had straight brown hair, I said, and was wearing a brown coat, and two or three people looked at me strangely and moved off. I'm sorry, I said to a man, and I laughed, and moved off. I'm dead, I said to several people and started to push them over, I'm dead, thank you, I said, thank you, please, I said, I'm dead, until two or three of them got hold of my arms and hustled me out. I'm sorry, I said, I couldn't come because of the accident. I'm sorry. Excuse me.

(*The Girl At The Party is lowered to the floor by two of the men and then all fall down except the actor who played the Fourth Interviewer. He remains seated as a Psychiatrist. The Third Applicant, on the floor, props his head up on his elbow and speaks to the audience.*)

THIRD APPLICANT. Can you help me, Doctor, I asked him.

(*The Psychiatrist crosses his legs and assumes a professional expression.*)

THIRD APPLICANT. Well, it started, well it started, I said, when I was sitting in front of the television set with my feet on the coffee table. Now I've sat there hundreds of times, thousands maybe, with a can of beer in my hand. I like to have a can of beer in my hand when I watch the beer ads. But now for no reason I can think of, the ad was making me sick. So I used the remote control to get to another channel, but each channel made me just as sick. The television was one thing and I was a person, and I was going to be sick. So I turned it off and had a panicky moment. I smelled the beer in my hand and as I vomited I

looked around the living room for something to grab on
to, something to look at, but there was just our new furniture. I tried to get a hold of myself. I tried to stare straight
ahead above the television set, at a little spot on the wall
I know. I've had little moments like that before, Doctor,
I said, panicky little moments like that when the earth
seems to slip out from under, and everything whirls around
and you try to hold onto something, some object, some
thought, but I couldn't think of anything. Later the panic
went away, I told him, it went away, and I'm much better
now. But I don't feel like doing anything anymore, except
sit and stare at the wall. I've lost my job. Katherine thought
I should come and see you. Can you help me, Doctor, I
asked him.

PSYCHIATRIST
Blah, blah, blah, blah, blah, blah, HOSTILE.
Blah, blah, blah, blah, blah, blah, PENIS.
Blah, blah, blah, blah, blah, blah, MOTHER.
    (holding out his hand)
Blah, blah, blah, blah, blah, blah, MONEY.

(The Third Applicant takes the Psychiatrist's hand and
gets up, extending his left hand to the next actor. This
begins a grand right and left with all the actors all over
the stage.)

ALL (chanting as they do the grand right and left).
Blah, blah, blah, blah, blah, blah, HOSTILE.
Blah, blah, blah, blah, blah, blah, PENIS.
Blah, blah, blah, blah, blah, blah, MOTHER.
Blah, blah, blah, blah, blah, blah, MONEY.
Blah, blah, blah, blah, blah, blah, HOSTILE.

Blah, blah, blah, blah, blah, blah, PENIS.
Blah, blah, blah, blah, blah, blah, MOTHER.
Blah, blah, blah, blah, blah, blah, MONEY.
(*forming couples and locking hands with arms crossed,
continuing to move, but in a smaller circle*)
Blah, blah, blah, blah, blah, blah, blah.
Blah, blah, blah, blah, blah, blah, blah.

(*Now they slow down to the speed of a church proces-
sion. The women bow their heads, letting their hair fall
forward over their faces. The "blah, blah, blah" continues, but much more slowly while some of the women
accompany it with a descant of "Kyrie Eleison." After
they have gone around in a circle once this way, the
actor who played the Fourth Interviewer sits with his
back to the audience as a Priest. The First Applicant
kneels next to him, facing the audience as if in a con-
fessional booth. The other six actors are at the back of
the stage in two lines, swaying slightly, heads down. The
women are in front with their hair still down over their
faces.*)

FIRST APPLICANT (*crossing himself perfunctorily and starting
to speak; his manner is not impassioned; it is clear that he
comes regularly to repeat this always fruitless ritual*).   Can
you help me, Father, I said, as I usually do, and he said,
as usual, nothing. I'm your friend, the housepainter, I said,
the good housepainter. Remember me, Father? He con-
tinued, as usual, to say nothing. Almost the only color you
get to paint these days, Father, I said, is white. Only white,
Father, I said, not expecting any more from him than usual,
but going on anyway. The color I really like to paint,
Father, is red, I said. Pure brick red. Now there's a con-

fession, Father. He said nothing. I'd like to take a trip to the country, Father, I said, and paint a barn door red, thinking that would get a rise out of him, but it didn't. God, I said then, deliberately taking the Lord's name in vain, the result of taking a three-inch brush and lightly kissing a coat of red paint on a barn door is something stunning and beautiful to behold. He still said nothing. Father, I said, springing it on him, Father, I'd like to join a monastery. My wife's sister, she could take care of the kids. Still nothing. Father, I said again, I'd like to join a monastery. Can you help me, Father? Nothing. Father, I said, I've tried lots of things in my life, I've gone in a lot of different directions, Father, and none of them seems any better than any other, Father, I said. Can you help me, Father, I said. But he said nothing as usual, and then, as usual, I went away.

(*The First Applicant and the Fourth Interviewer, who haven't moved at all during the confession, move upstage to join the others as the music starts up violently in a rock beat. The actors do a rock version of the Virginia reel.*)

SECOND INTERVIEWER (*loudly*).   My

(*All bow to partners.*)

FOURTH APPLICANT (*loudly*).   fault.

(*All dos-à-dos.*)

SECOND APPLICANT (*loudly*).   Excuse

(*All circle around.*)

FOURTH INTERVIEWER (*loudly*).   me.

(*All peel off.*)

FIRST INTERVIEWER (*loudly*).   Can you

SECOND APPLICANT (*loudly*).   help

FIRST APPLICANT (*loudly*).   me?

FOURTH INTERVIEWER (*loudly*).   Next.

(*All continue dancing, joining hands at the center to form a revolving door again. They repeat the preceding eight speeches. Then the Second Interviewer speaks rapidly, as a Square Dance Caller.*)

SQUARE DANCE CALLER.   Step right up, ladies and gents, and shake the hand of the next governor of this state. Shake his hand and say hello. Tell your friends you shook the hand of the next governor of the state. Step right up and shake his hand. Ask him questions. Tell him problems. Say hello. Step right up, shake his hand, shake the hand, ladies and gents, of the next governor of the state. Tell your folks: I shook his hand. When he's famous you'll be proud. Step right up, ladies and gents, and shake his hand. Ask him questions. Tell him problems. Say hello. Step right up, ladies and gents. Don't be shy. Shake the hand of the next governor of this state.

(*The actors have formed a crowd, downstage right, facing the audience. They give the impression of being but a few of a great number of people, all trying to squeeze*

to the front to see and speak to the political candidate.
The Fourth Interviewer, now playing a Politician, stands
on a box, stage left, facing the audience. The Second
Interviewer stands by the crowd and keeps it in order.)

POLITICIAN. Thank you very much, I said cheerfully, and
good luck to you, I said, turning my smile to the next one.

(The First Interviewer, panting as the Girl At The Party,
squeezes out of the crowd and rushes up to the Politician,
who smiles at her benignly.)

POLITICIAN. Our children ARE our most important asset, I
agreed earnestly. Yes they are, I said solemnly. Children,
I said, with a long pause, are our most important asset. I
only wish I could, madame, I said earnestly, standing tall,
but rats, I said regretfully, are a city matter.

(The First Interviewer returns to the crowd while the
Third Interviewer, as the Telephone Operator, rushes up
to the Politician. She appeals to him, making the same
noise she made when her stomach hurt her.)

POLITICIAN. Nobody knows more about red tape than I do,
I said knowingly, and I wish you luck, I said, turning my
smile to the next one.

(The Third Interviewer returns to the crowd and the
Fourth Applicant goes up to the Politician.)

POLITICIAN. I certainly will, I said, with my eyes sparkling,
taking a pencil out of my pocket. And what's your name,

I said, looking at her sweetly and signing my name at the same time. That's a lovely name, I said.

(*The Fourth Applicant returns to the crowd while the Third Applicant, as an Older Man, shakes the Politician's hand.*)

POLITICIAN.   Yes sir, I said, those were the days. And good luck to you, sir, I said respectfully but heartily, and look out for the curb, I said, turning my smile to the next one.

(*The Third Applicant returns to the crowd and the Second Applicant approaches the Politician.*)

POLITICIAN.   Indeed yes, the air we breathe ɪs foul, I said indignantly. I agree with you entirely, I said wholeheartedly. And if my opponent wins it's going to get worse, I said with conviction. We'd all die within ten years, I said. And good luck to you, madame, I said politely, and turned my smile to the next one.

(*The First Applicant approaches him, his cap in his hand.*)

POLITICIAN.   Well, I said confidingly, getting a bill through the legislature is easier said than done, and answering violence, I said warningly, with violence, I said earnestly, is not the answer, and how do you do, I said, turning my smile to the next one.

(*Next, two Sighing Lovers—we saw them on Fourteenth Street—played by the First and Second Interviewers, approach the Politician.*)

POLITICIAN.   No, I said, I never said my opponent would kill us all. No, I said, I never said that. May the best man win, I said manfully.

(*Half-hearted cheers. The First and Second Interviewers return to the crowd.*)

POLITICIAN.   I do feel, I said without false modesty, that I'm better qualified in the field of foreign affairs than my opponents are, yes, I said, BUT, I said, with a pause for emphasis, foreign policy is the business of the President, not the Governor, therefore I will say nothing about the war, I said with finality.

(*The crowd makes a restive sound, then freezes.*)

POLITICIAN.   Do you want us shaking hands, I asked the photographer, turning my profile to the left. Goodbye, I said cheerfully, and good luck to you too.

(*The crowd makes a louder protest, then freezes.*)

POLITICIAN.   I'm sorry, I said seriously, but I'll have to study that question a good deal more before I can answer it.

(*The crowd makes an angry noise, then freezes.*)

POLITICIAN.   Of course, I said frowning, we must all support the President, I said as I turned concernedly to the next one.

(*The crowd makes a very angry sound, then freezes.*)

POLITICIAN. I'm sorry about the war, I said. Nobody could be sorrier than I am, I said sorrowfully. But I'm afraid, I said gravely, that there are no easy answers.

(*smiles, pleased with himself*)

Good luck to you too, I said cheerfully, and turned my smile to the next one.

(*The Politician topples from his box, beginning his speech all over again. Simultaneously, all the other actors lurch about the stage, speaking again in character: the Shopper On Fourteenth Street, the Gym Instructor, the Subway Rider, the Telephone Operator, the Girl At The Party, the Analysand, and the Housepainter. Simultaneously, they all stop and freeze, continue again, freeze again, then continue with music under. The Second Interviewer, acting as policeman, begins to line them up in a diagonal line, like marching dolls, one behind the other. As they are put into line they begin to move their mouths without sound, like fish in a tank. The music stops. When all are in line the Second Interviewer joins them.*)

SECOND INTERVIEWER.   My

FOURTH APPLICANT.   fault.

SECOND APPLICANT.   Excuse

FOURTH INTERVIEWER.   me.

FIRST INTERVIEWER.   Can you

SECOND APPLICANT.   help

FIRST APPLICANT. me?

FOURTH INTERVIEWER. Next.

(All continue marching in place, moving their mouths, and shouting their lines as the lights come slowly down.)

SECOND INTERVIEWER. My

FOURTH APPLICANT. fault.

SECOND APPLICANT. Excuse

FOURTH INTERVIEWER. me.

FIRST INTERVIEWER. Can you

SECOND APPLICANT. help

FIRST APPLICANT. me?

FOURTH INTERVIEWER. Next.

TV

The youth Narcissus mistook his own reflection in the water for another person ... He was numb. He had adapted to his extension of himself and had become a closed system.

Marshall McLuhan

TV was premiered as part of the AMERICA HURRAH production at the Pocket Theatre in New York City.

The cast:

Conard Fowkes as Hal

Brenda Smiley as Susan

Bill Macy as George

Ronnie Gilbert as Helen Fargis, the President's wife, a UGP researcher, a member of the rock and roll group, a peace marcher, Lily Heaven, the headache sufferer, a singer in the evangelist choir, and Mother in "My Favorite Teenager"

Henry Calvert as Harry Fargis, First News Announcer, Steve, the President, a UGP researcher, a member of the rock and roll group, Weather Announcer, He in the Billion Dollar Movie, Evangelist, and Father in "My Favorite Teenager"

James Barbosa   as Wonderboy, Second News Announcer, the man in the cigarette commercial, Bill, UGP Announcer, a member of the rock and roll group, one young man from New York City, Lily Heaven's Announcer, Ron Campbell, Johnny Holland, and a singer in the evangelist choir

Cynthia Harris   as the woman in the cigarette commercial, the President's older daughter, a UGP researcher, a member of the rock and roll group, a peace marcher, Famous Television Personality, Carol, She in the Billion Dollar Movie, and a singer in the evangelist choir

Joyce Aaron   as Sally, the President's younger daughter, the Spanish teacher, a UGP researcher, a member of the rock and roll group, Annie Kappelhoff, Lady Announcer, Luci, a singer in the evangelist choir, and Daughter in "My Favorite Teenager"

Slides: drawings by Francisca Duran-Reynals
       photographs by Phill Niblock and Martin Bough

Make-up: Remy Charlip

Design for printed script: Sharon Thie

The set is white and impersonal. There are two doors on the stage right wall: one leads to the rest rooms, the other to the hall.

Downstage right is the control console in a television viewing room. It faces the audience.

Above the console, also facing the audience, is a screen. Projected on it, from the rear, is the logo of a television station.

Downstage left is a water cooler, a closet for coats, and a telephone. Downstage right is a bulletin board. Upstage center is a table with a coffee maker on it.

Hal and Susan are seated at the console, Susan in the middle chair. They are both in their twenties. Hal is playing, as he often will, with his penknife: whittling pencils, paring his nails, or throwing it at the bulletin board. Susan is involved with the papers on the console, with sharpening pencils, and so forth.

At the back of the stage, on the left, are the five actors who will portray what will appear on television. For the moment they have no light on them and their backs are to the audience.

To indicate the correlation of the events and dialogue on television with those which occur in the viewing room, the play is printed in two columns.

HAL
So what do you say?

SUSAN
I don't know.

HAL
That doesn't get us very far, does it?

SUSAN

Well it's such a surprise, your asking. I was planning to work on my apartment.

HAL

I'll help you, after the movie.

SUSAN

That's too late. One thing I have to have is eight hours' sleep. I really have to have that.

(*George enters; he is older than Hal and Susan, and is in charge of the viewing room.*)

HAL

Hi, George.

SUSAN

Hello, George.

GEORGE (*to Susan*)

Is that a new dress?

SUSAN (*nodding toward Hal*)

HE didn't even notice.

(George *puts his coat
and jacket in the closet
and puts on a cardigan
sweater.*)

GEORGE
How many check marks
have you made, Hal?

HAL
I don't know, George. I
don't count.

SUSAN
I got it on Fourteenth
Street. I love going into
places like that because
they're so cheap.

GEORGE
If you don't make at least
a hundred check marks,
they'll dock you. That's
what the totals count col-
umn is for.

SUSAN (*looking at herself in
a mirror*)
Have I lost any weight?

GEORGE
Where would you lose it
from?

HAL

George, how come they haven't asked us for a detailed report in nearly three weeks?

GEORGE

How should I know?

HAL

Think they're forgetting about us, George?

SUSAN

I was trying to tell in the Ladies, but the fluorescent light in there just burns your eyes.

HAL

I've never been to the Ladies. You think I'd like it?

GEORGE

This viewing room is the backbone of the rating system.

HAL

He said that to you LAST month, George. Things move fast.

GEORGE
Are you trying to make
me nervous?

HAL
Maybe.

GEORGE
Well don't, because my
stomach is not very good
this morning.

SUSAN
I want to know seriously,
and I mean seriously, do
you think I've lost any
weight?

GEORGE
Where from?

HAL
Why don't you let your-
self go?

SUSAN
What do you mean?

HAL
Just let nature take its
course.

SUSAN
What if nature wants you
to be a big fat slob?

HAL
Then be a big fat slob.

SUSAN
Thanks.

(Hal, Susan, and George sit down and get ready for the day's work. George turns a dial on the console which turns on TV. Two of the People On Television turn around to play Helen and Harry Fargis.

All of the People On Television are dressed in shades of gray. They make no costume changes and use no real props. Their faces are made up with thin horizontal black lines to suggest the way they might appear to a viewer. They are playing television images. Their style of acting is cool, not pushy. As television characters, they have only a few facial masks, such as "cute," "charming," or "serious," which they use infallibly, like signals, in the course of each television segment.

After each television segment, the People involved in it will freeze where they are until it is time for them to become another character.

As the play progresses, the People On Television will use more and more of the stage. The impression should be that of a slow invasion of the viewing room. Hal, Susan, and George will simply move around the People On Tele-

vision when that becomes necessary. Ultimately, the control console itself will be taken over by television characters, so that the distinction between what is on television and what is occurring in the viewing room will be lost completely.

The attention of the audience should be focused not on a parody of television, but on the relationship of the life that appears on television to the life that goes on in the viewing room.

All of the actors will need to be constantly aware of what is happening on all parts of the stage, in order to give and take the attention of the audience to and from each other, and also in order to demonstrate the influence of the style of certain television segments on the behavior of Hal, Susan, and George.)

(*Slide on screen: Wonderboy's face.*)

HAL
Why try to look like somebody else?

(*Helen and Harry Fargis are at home. Helen is baking cookies.*)

HELEN
Harry, what are you working on in the garage?

SUSAN
I'm trying to look like myself, thin. Very thin.

HARRY
If I succeed in my experiments, nobody in the world will be hungry for love. Ever again.

HAL (*offering him one*)
Want a cigarette, George?

GEORGE
No, thanks.

HELEN
Hungry for love? Harry, you make me nervous.

HAL
Just one?

HELEN
You really do.

GEORGE
No.

HARRY
Men will put down their arms.

SUSAN
Hal, why don't you try to help George instead of being so cruel?

HELEN
You haven't been to work for a week now. You'll lose your job.

HAL
I'm just offering him a cigarette.

HARRY
You don't understand.
This is more important.

HELEN
Oh, Harry. I don't under-
stand you at all any more.
I really don't.

GEORGE (*as Hal takes the
    cigarette away*)
Give me one.

SUSAN
Hal, that's utter torture
for George.

(*Harry goes back to the
garage. Helen mumbles
to herself as she cleans
up the kitchen.*)

HELEN
I don't know.

GEORGE
Give me one.

HELEN
I just don't know. He used
to be so docile.

SUSAN
Don't, George. He's just
playing cat and mouse.

HELEN
And now I just don't
know—

HARRY (*calling from garage*)
Helen!

HELEN
Harry?

HAL
That's right, George. Don't have one. I'm just playing cat and mouse.
(*lights a cigarette*)

HARRY
Helen, my experiments.

HELEN
Harry, what?

GEORGE
Just give it to me, will you?

HARRY
A terrible mistake.

SUSAN
Try to control yourself for just another half hour, George.

HELEN
Harry, your voice—

GEORGE
No.

SUSAN
Why not?

HARRY (*his voice getting lower and gruffer*)
For the love of heaven, Helen, keep away from me.

GEORGE

Because I don't wanna control myself for just another half hour.

HAL

Whatever you want, George.
(*hands a cigarette to George*)

HELEN

What happened?

HARRY

I can't restrain myself anymore. I'm coming through the garage door.
(*comes through the garage door, wearing a monster mask; his voice is now very deep and gruff*)
I'm irresistibly attracted to you, Helen, irresistibly.

HELEN

Eeeeeeeeeeeeeeeeeeeeek!

HARRY (*stepping toward her*)

Helen, I love you.
(*goes to embrace her*)

HELEN

Harry, you're hideous. Eeeeek! Eeeeeeeeeeeek! Eeeeeeeeeeeeek!

(*As Helen screams, Wonderboy is discovered, in mufti, doing his homework.*)

SUSAN

What was the point of that, Hal?

HAL

No point.

WONDERBOY

Two superquantums plus five uranium neutrons, and I've got the mini-sub fuel. Hooray. Boy, will my friends in the U.S. Navy be pleased. Hey, what's that? Better use my wonder-vision. Helen Fargis seems to be in trouble. Better change to Wonderboy.

(*as if throwing open his shirt*)

And fly over there in a flash.

(*jumping as if flying*)

I guess I'm in the nick of time.

(*with one super-powerful punch in the jaw he subdues Harry, the monster*)

HELEN

Oh, Wonderboy, what would have happened if you hadn't come? But what will happen to ɪᴛ?

WONDERBOY

I'll fly him to a distant zoo where they'll take good care of him.

HELEN

Oh, Wonderboy, how can I ever repay you?

WONDERBOY

Are those home-baked cookies I smell?

SUSAN

The president of the company has an Eames chair.

(*Helen smiles at Wonderboy through her tears; he puts his arm around her shoulders.*)

WONDERBOY

Tune in tomorrow, boys and girls, when I'll subdue a whole country full of monsters.

GEORGE

How do you know that?

(*Slide: "Winners Eat Wondrex."*)

SUSAN
Jennifer showed it to me.

GEORGE
You asked to see it?

SUSAN
Don't worry George. He wasn't there. I just had this crazy wild impulse as I was passing his office. I wanted to see what it looked like. Isn't that wild?

HAL
Did you sit in it?

WONDERBOY
And in the meantime, remember: winners eat Wondrex.
(*smiles and jumps in the air, as if flying away*)

(*Slide: little girls with shopping bags.*)

FIRST NEWS ANNOUNCER
Little girls with big shopping bags means back to school season is here again. Among the many shoppers in downtown New York were Darlene, nine, Lila, four, and Lucy Gladden, seven, of Lynbrook, Long Island.

(*Slide: the Vice President.*)

FIRST NEWS ANNOUNCER
In Washington, D.C., as he left John Foster Dulles Airport, as President Johnson's favorite

(*Slide: second view of the Vice President.*)

NIBLOCK/BOUGH

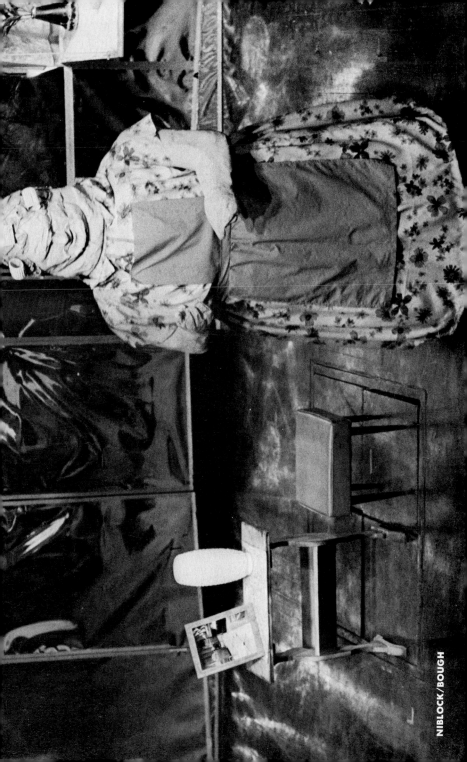

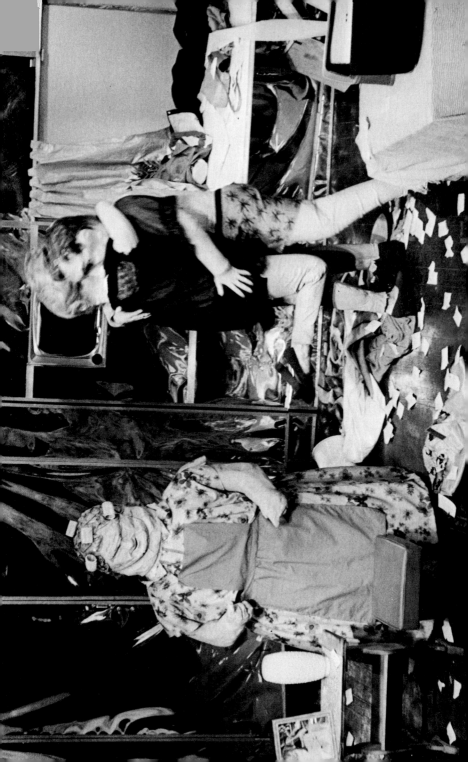

FIRST NEWS ANNOUNCER
representative, the Vice
President said he was
bursting with confidence.

SUSAN
I didn't dare. What would
I have said if he'd come
in?

(*George goes to the
rest room.*)

(*Slide: first view of
Vietnamese mourners.*)

HAL
I love you, Mr. President
of my great big company,
and that's why I'm sitting
in your nice warm leather
arm chair.

SUSAN
You're perverted. I don't
want to be a person work-
ing in a company who's
never seen her president.

SECOND NEWS ANNOUNCER
U.S. spokesmen in Saigon
said families would be
given adequate shelter and
compensation. Our planes
are under strict orders not
to return to base with any
bombs. The United States
regrets that a friendly village was hit. The native
toll was estimated at sixty.

SUSAN (*to Hal, who has got-
     ten up*)
  While you're up—

HAL
  What?

SUSAN
  You know. Get me a
  Coke.
     (*titters at her own
     joke*)

     (*Hal goes out through
     the hall door. George
     returns from the rest
     room.*)

(*Slide: second view of
Vietnamese mourners.*)

SECOND NEWS ANNOUNCER
  This was high, explained
  spokesmen, in answer to
  questions, because of the
  type of bomb dropped.
  These are known as Lazy
  Dogs. Each Lazy Dog
  bomb contains ten thou-
  sand slivers of razor-sharp
  steel.

     (*Slide: third view of
     Vietnamese mourners.*)

GEORGE (*turning TV sound
     off*)
  Can I come over tonight?

(*Volume off.*)

(*Slide: a pack of Long-
ford cigarettes superim-
posed on a lake.*)

SUSAN

Not tonight.
  (*goes to bulletin board*)

(*Two People On Tele-
vision do a silent com-
mercial for Longford
cigarettes: a man lights
a woman's cigarette and
she looks pleased.*)

GEORGE (*following her*)
Why not tonight?

SUSAN

Because I don't feel like
it.

GEORGE

You have a date?

SUSAN

What business is that of
yours? Don't think be-
cause—

GEORGE

Who with?

SUSAN

None of your business.

GEORGE

What about late, after
you get back, like one
o'clock?

SUSAN
That's too late. I need
lots of sleep.

GEORGE
I'll call first.

SUSAN
You'd better.

(*Whenever Hal, Susan,
and George have noth-
ing else to do, they stare
straight ahead, as if at
a television screen.
George and Susan do
this now. Hal comes
back with two Cokes.
George goes to the tele-
phone and dials it.*)

(*Slide on the screen:
"The Endless Fron-
tier."*)

GEORGE
Hello, dear. Yes, I'm here.
Listen, I'm afraid I have
to take the midnight to
three shift.

(*Sally and Bill are two
characters in the West-
ern.*)

(*Hal turns TV volume
on.*)

SALLY
Don't go, Bill.

BILL
I've got to.

GEORGE
I've got to. The night su-
pervisor is out.

SALLY
Oh, Bill.

GEORGE
And I've already said I
would.

(*Bill leaves.*)

SALLY
Oh, Bill.

GEORGE
Listen, let's talk about it
over dinner, huh? I'll be
out after you go to sleep
and in before you wake
up so what's the differ-
ence? Listen, let's talk
about it over dinner, I
said. Listen, I love you.
Goodbye.
    (*hangs up*)

(*Sally fixes her hair in
the mirror.*)

HAL (*watching TV intently
but talking to George*)
You have to take the mid-
night to three shift,
George? That's really too
bad.

(*Sally is surprised by
Steve, the villain, who
has just been waiting
for Bill to ride off.*)

SALLY
Steve!

HAL
Got a call while I was out?

STEVE
Bill's dead, Sally.

SALLY
I don't believe you.

GEORGE (*snapping* TV *volume off*)
Do either of you want to take on some evening overtime this week?

SUSAN
Which?

GEORGE
Five to midnight Tuesday and Thursday.

HAL
Thursday.

SUSAN
Oh, all right, I'll take Tuesday.

HAL
Did you want Thursday?

SUSAN
I'd like to get the apartment finished.

(*Volume off.*)

(*Steve tries to embrace Sally. She slaps him hard as he approaches her. He tries it again. She slaps him again. He tries it a third time. She gets him a third time. Then he grabs and kisses her despite her terrible struggling.*)

HAL
Then give me Tuesday.

SUSAN
Not if you HAVE some-
thing on Thursday.

HAL
No sweat.

SUSAN
Oh, I know. It was that
talk with that man.

*(Bill, his arm wounded,
appears again. Seeing
Steve with Sally, he
draws and aims.)*

*(Hal turns TV volume
on.)*

BILL
Sally, duck!

GEORGE *(snapping TV vol-
ume off)*
What talk with what
man?

(Volume off.)

SUSAN
A man he has to talk to.

*(Sally ducks. Bill shoots
Steve, then goes to Sally
to make sure she's all
right. Steve, however, is
not badly wounded and
he reaches for Bill's
gun. The gun falls to
the floor and they fight.
Sally tries to get into
the fight, but is pushed
away.)*

GEORGE
About a job?

HAL
I probably won't even see
him.

GEORGE
What kind of job?

HAL
For the government. I tell
you I probably won't see
him.

GEORGE
If you quit, Hal, I'll need
three weeks' notice. If you
care about severance pay.

HAL (*turning TV volume
on*)
I haven't seen him yet,
even.

(*Bill is losing his fight
with Steve because of
his wounded arm. Steve
is about to get the gun.*)

GEORGE
Or about me.

SALLY (*warningly*)
Bill!

HAL
I wasn't going to mention
it.

SUSAN
I'm sorry. It was my fault.

GEORGE (*turning volume off*)
Just don't spring anything
on me If you don't like
the job, leave. But don't
spring anything on me

(*Volume off.*)

(*In the nick of time,
Sally shoots Steve in the
back with a rifle. As he*

because I can't take it,
you know that.

*falls he makes a mute
appeal to her. He is
dead now and she is ap-
palled at what she's
done.)*

HAL

George, I'm NOT quitting.

SUSAN

He likes this job too
much, George.

HAL

I love it more than my
own life. I wouldn't leave
it for all the world. Honest Injun, George.
  (*turns volume on*)

SALLY (*embracing Bill*)
  Oh, Bill!

GEORGE

Can you imagine what I'd
have to go through to
train another person? Can
you?

BILL
  I love you, Sally.

SALLY (*touched*)
  Oh, Bill.

BILL
  Let's move to another
  town.

SALLY (*delighted*)
Oh Bill.

(*Bill and Sally ride off
together into the dusk.*)

SUSAN

Listen, I just remembered
a joke. There's this writing on the subway. "I love
grills" it says on the wall.
So somebody crosses out
"grills" and writes in
"girls." "I love girls" it
says now. And then some-
body else writes in,
"What about us grills?"
(*laughs and laughs over
this*)

(*Slide: the President
and his family.*)

SECOND NEWS ANNOUNCER

SUSAN

What about us grills?
Isn't that fantastic?

The President is accom-
panied by his wife, Lady
Bird Johnson, and by his
two daughters, Lynda
Bird Johnson and Luci
Baines Johnson Nugent,
who lives in nearby Austin
with her husband Patrick
Nugent, President John-
son's son-in-law.

(*Slide: second view of the President and his family.*)

HAL
What's the matter with you?

(*The President appears at a podium reading a speech. He is indeed accompanied by his wife and daughters.*)

(*Slide: the President alone.*)

SUSAN (*still laughing*)
I think that's the funniest thing I ever heard.

HAL
Shhhh.

PRESIDENT
We will stamp out aggression wherever and whenever.

(*Susan continues laughing.*)

HAL
Shhhhh. Stop it.

SUSAN
I can't.

PRESIDENT
We will tighten our defenses and fight, to guarantee the peace of our children, our children's children, and their children.

SUSAN
I can't stop. Get the water.

(George gets up to get some water. Hal wants to watch TV and can't hear it at all because of Susan's laughter.)

PRESIDENT
That all men are not well-intentioned or well-informed or even basically good, is unfortunate.

HAL
This is easier.
(slaps Susan very hard on the face)

SUSAN
Ow!

PRESIDENT
But these people will not be indulged.

SUSAN
Just who do you think you are!

(Applause by the President's family. No sound in this play need be put on tape; all of it can be provided by the People On Television.)

HAL
Are you finished?

SUSAN
I couldn't help it.

PRESIDENT
Those who are our friends will declare themselves publicly. The others, we will not tolerate.

SUSAN
Sadist.

(*Slide: second view of the President alone.*)

PRESIDENT
Belief in American success and victory is the cornerstone of our faith.

SUSAN
Why didn't anyone get water?

GEORGE
Don't look at me.

PRESIDENT
Whatever else may chance to happen on far-off shores, nothing, I repeat nothing, will be allowed to disturb the serenity of our cities and suburbs, and when we fight we fight for a safer and more comfortable America, now and in years to come. Thank you.

SUSAN

You don't slap people be-
cause they're sick.

HAL

Every day we go through
the same thing. You
laugh. We bring you wa-
ter. You spill the water all
over everybody, and half
an hour later you stop.

SUSAN

Give   me   the   water,
George. I'm going to take
a pill.

GEORGE

What makes you laugh
like that?

(*Hal lowers the volume
but does not turn it
off.*)

(*Slide: third view of the
President and his fam-
ily.*)

SECOND NEWS ANNOUNCER

The President and his
family will now be cheered
by the cadet corps.

(*The President and his
family respond to cheers
like mechanical dolls.
Turning his back, the
Second News An-
nouncer provides us
with one hummed bar
of "So Hello Lyn-
don."*)

(*A Spanish Teacher ap-
pears.*)

(*Slide: the Spanish
Teacher's face.*)

(*Volume low.*)

SUSAN

I'm a hysteric. I mean I'm not constantly hysterical but sometimes I get that way. I react that way, through my body. You're a compulsive, Hal, a nasty little compulsive.

HAL (*turning volume off*)
How do you know?

SUSAN

I've discussed it with my analyst. Hysterics react through their bodies. Compulsives react compulsively.

GEORGE
What does he say about me?

SUSAN
He doesn't.

GEORGE
Hmph.

HAL
How long have you been going now? Twenty-seven years?

SPANISH TEACHER

Buenos dias muchachos and muchachas. **Hello,** boys and girls. Muchachos. Boys. Muchachas. Girls. Aqui es la casa. Here is the house. Casa. House.

(*Volume off.*)

(*The Spanish Teacher finishes the lesson.*)

(*Efficient researchers walk back and forth across the stage, checking things, nodding at each other curtly, and so on.*)

(*Slide: the efficient researchers.*)

SUSAN
A year, wise guy.

HAL
How long do you expect
to be going?

SUSAN
It might take another two
or three years.

GEORGE
I know people who have
gone for ten or twelve
years.

HAL
Don't you think that's a
lot?

GEORGE
If you need it, you need
it. It's a sickness like any
other sickness. It's got to
be looked after.

HAL
What did they do in the
old days?

GEORGE (*turning volume up*)   (*Volume up.*)
They stayed sick.

UGP ANNOUNCER
Who are they? They are

a community of devotion.

(Slide: "UGP" in very Germanic lettering.)

UGP ANNOUNCER
Men and women whose lives are dedicated to the researching of more perfect products for you. Get the benefit of a community of devotion. Look for the letters UGP whenever you buy a car, radio, television set, or any of a thousand other products. Their tool: devotion. Their goal: perfection.

(Slide: a civil rights demonstration.)

SUSAN
My analyst has been going to HIS analyst for twenty-five years.

HAL
How do you know?

SUSAN
He told me.

FIRST NEWS ANNOUNCER
Three men were critically injured during a civil

rights demonstration in Montgomery, Alabama today.

GEORGE
Can you feel the tranquilizer working?

SUSAN
A little bit. I think so.

(Slide: the Vice President.)

FIRST NEWS ANNOUNCER
This afternoon the Vice President arrived in Honolulu. As he stepped off the plane he told newsmen things are looking up.

GEORGE
Maybe I should have one too.

(Slide: a map of China.)

FIRST NEWS ANNOUNCER
The Defense Department today conceded that United States aircraft may have mistakenly flown over Chinese territory last month. It regrets the incident.

SUSAN *(turning volume off.)*
Are you upset?

(Volume off.)

GEORGE
I can feel my stomach.

SUSAN (*reaching into her bag to give him a pill*)
Here.

GEORGE
I'd like some coffee.

HAL
I'd like some lunch.

SUSAN
Lunch! I'll get it.
(*dashes into her coat and is almost out the door*)

HAL
Hey!

SUSAN
Rare with onion and a danish. I know. So long, you guys.

HAL (*throwing his penknife into the bulletin board*)
Think she's all right?

(*Slide: a rock and roll group.*)

(*A rock and roll group is seen singing and playing.*)

GEORGE

People wouldn't say this
was a crazy office or anything like that.

HAL

Nope.

GEORGE

She's really a nice girl,
isn't she?

HAL (*doing calisthenics*)
Yup.

GEORGE

You like her, don't you?

HAL

Yup.

GEORGE

I mean you don't just
think she's a good lay, do
you?

HAL

What makes you think I
lay her?

GEORGE

Well, don't you?

HAL
>George, that's an old
trick.

GEORGE
>I'm just trying to find out
if you really like her.

HAL
>Why do you care?

GEORGE
>I feel protective.

HAL
>That's right. She's half
your age, isn't she?

GEORGE
>Not exactly half.

HAL
>How old are you, George,
exactly?

GEORGE
>Forty-three.

HAL (*crossing to water
cooler*)
>Humph.

GEORGE
>What's that mean?

HAL

I was just wondering what
it was like to be forty-
three.

GEORGE

It stinks.

HAL

That's what I thought.

GEORGE

You'll be forty-three
sooner than you think.

HAL

I'll never be forty-three.

GEORGE

Why not?

HAL

I don't intend to live that
long.

*(The rock and roll
group bows.)*

GEORGE

You have something?

*(Slide: a group of peace
marchers.)*

HAL

No. I just don't intend to
live that long.
   *(returns to console and
   turns volume on)*

*(A group of peace
marchers appears.)*

FIRST NEWS ANNOUNCER
A group of so-called peaceniks marched down the center mall of the capital today, singing:

(*The peace marchers sing "We Shall Overcome."*)

GEORGE (*sits*)
You're probably a socialist.

HAL
A socialist?

GEORGE
A socialist at twenty and a Republican at forty. Everybody goes through that cycle.

FIRST NEWS ANNOUNCER
One young man from New York City predicted:

ONE YOUNG MAN FROM NEW YORK CITY
The Washington Monument's going to burst into bloom and—

(*It is as if the sound were cut off on the word he was going to say, but we can read "Fuck" on his lips.*)

GEORGE
It's healthy.

(*Slide: Annie Kappel-hoff.*)

FIRST NEWS ANNOUNCER
A little girl, Annie Kappelhoff, had her own opinion:

ANNIE (*as if leading a cheer*)
Burn yourselves, not your draft cards, burn yourselves, not your draft cards—

(*The sound is cut off on Annie, too, as she continues the same cheer.*)

FIRST NEWS ANNOUNCER
Later in the day Annie was the star of her own parade. She's head-cheerleader of Wilumet High School in Maryland. Today Annie cheered her team on to victory, thirty to nothing, over neighboring South Dearing. Annie is also an ardent supporter of the young American

Nazi party, and hopes to
become a model. And
now, a message.

(*Slide: a jar of K-F
soap-cream.*)

HAL
Are you a Republican,
George?

FAMOUS TV PERSONALITY
Are you one of those lucky
women who has all the
time in the world?

GEORGE
That's right.

HAL
You know I have a lot of
friends who won't even
speak to Republicans.

GEORGE
I'd rather not discuss politics.

FAMOUS TV PERSONALITY
Or are you like most of
us: busy, busy, busy all
day long with home or job
so that when evening
comes you hardly have
time to wash your face,
much less transform your-
self into the living doll
he loves.

HAL
Why not?

GEORGE
Because we probably
don't see eye to eye.

HAL
So?

GEORGE
So I'd rather not discuss
it. And my stomach's up-
set.

FAMOUS TV PERSONALITY
Well then, K-F is for you.
More than a soap. More
than a cream. It's a soap-
cream. You apply it in
less time than it takes to
wash your face and it
leaves your skin tingling
with loveliness. Try it.
And for an extra super
thrill, use it in the shower.

(Slide: Lily Heaven.)

LILY HEAVEN'S ANNOUNCER
The Lily Heaven Show,
ladies and gentlemen,
starring that great star of
stage, screen, and television: Lily Heaven.

(Out through imagi-
nary curtains comes
Lily Heaven, very star-
like. She greets her au-
dience in her own inim-
itable way. She sings a
line from a popular
American love song.)

(There is a special
knock on the viewing
room door.)

HAL
What's that?

GEORGE
Nothing.

    (*George turns volume off.*)

    (*Volume off.*)

    (*Slide: a second view of Lily Heaven.*)

HAL
What do you mean, nothing?

GEORGE (*calling*)
One minute.

HAL (*getting panicky*)
One minute until what?

    (*George turns out the lights in the viewing room.*)

HAL
I knew it. What's going on?

GEORGE (*calling*)
Okay.

HAL
Okay what? What? What?

SUSAN (*coming through the
    door with a cake with
    lighted candles on it*)
Okay this, stupid.

HAL
    Oh my God, you're crazy.

SUSAN AND GEORGE
    One, two, three.
      (*singing*)
    Happy Birthday to you,
    Happy Birthday to you,
    Happy Birthday dear Ha-
    al,
    Happy Birthday to you.

      (*Susan kisses Hal on
      the lips.*)

SUSAN
    Happy Birthday. You had
    no idea, did you?

HAL
    No.

GEORGE
    Happy Birthday.

HAL
    Thanks a lot.

SUSAN
Make a wish and blow.

(*Hal blows on the can-
dles but doesn't get
them all.*)

SUSAN
Well, almost.

(*George turns the view-
ing room lights on
again, and Susan gets
two presents from the
closet.*)

SUSAN
People thought I was
crazy walking down the
hall with this cake and
this lunch in a paper bag.
And I was petrified one of
you would swing the door
open while I was waiting
in the corridor and knock
me down and the cake
and everything. I was al-
most sure you'd guessed,
Hal, when I put the pres-
ents in my locker this
morning.

HAL
I hadn't.

SUSAN
I love birthdays. I know
it's childish but I really
do. Look at the card on
George's.

HAL
It's cute.

SUSAN
Open it.

(*Hal opens the pack-
age. It's a tie.*)

HAL
Well thanks, George. I
can use this.
(*makes a mock noose
of it around his neck*)

GEORGE
You're welcome.

SUSAN (*looking at the label
as if she hadn't seen it
before*)
It's a good tie.

GEORGE
What'd you expect?

(*George is biting into
an egg salad sandwich.*

Hal starts to open the
second present.)

SUSAN (*stopping Hal*)
Save mine for when we
eat the cake, so the birthday will last longer.

HAL   (*Lily Heaven finishes*
George, there's egg salad   *singing and bows.*)
all over the dials.

GEORGE (*turning volume on*)   LILY HEAVEN
Sorry.   So long, everybody.

SUSAN
Here's a napkin. I'll make
some coffee.   LILY HEAVEN
                                This is Lily Heaven say-
                                ing so long.

GEORGE
Good.   (*Applause from part of*
                                Lily Heaven's audience,
                                played by the People
                                On Television, who
                                stand behind her.)

                                LILY HEAVEN (*as if each sen-*
                                tence were her last)
                                Here's wishing you a good
                                week before we meet
                                again. From all of us here

(*George and Hal are mesmerized by Lily Heaven. Susan is paying no attention but is fussing with the coffee things and putting paper bags, as party hats, on Hal and George.*)

GEORGE

Give me another of those tranquilizers, please. The first one doesn't seem to have done a thing.

to all of you out there: so long. Thanks a lot and God bless you. This is Lily signing off. I only hope that you enjoyed watching us as much as we enjoyed being here. So long. It's been wonderful being with you. Really grand, and I hope you'll invite us into your living room again next week. I only wish we could go on but I'm afraid it's time to say so long, so from the actors and myself, from the staff here, I want to wish you all a very very good week. This is your Lily saying so long to you. So long. So long. So long. So long. Have a happy, and so long. Till next week. Bye. So long. Bye. So long.

(*Slide: a weather map.*)

WEATHER ANNOUNCER
And now, the weather.

(Hal turns the volume   (Volume off.)
off. Susan has plugged
in the hot plate and
coffee maker. She also
has some real coffee and
a jar of dried cream,
some sugar and sugar
substitute in little bags
stolen from a lunch-
eonette, napkins and
little wooden stick-stir-
rers.)

HAL *(who has been opening*
his present)
Say, this is nice.

SUSAN
It's an art book.

HAL
I can see that.

GEORGE
Hal especially interested
in art?

SUSAN
A person doesn't have to
be especially interested in
art to like it.

HAL

It must have cost a lot,
Susan. Here, George.
(*passes George a piece
of cake*)

SUSAN

Well, as a matter of fact,
I got it on sale at Mar-
boro.

HAL

If I had a place for it
everything would be fine.
Cake, Susan?

SUSAN (*to George*)
Hal still doesn't have a
place.

(*Slide: Miracle Head-
ache Pills.*)

GEORGE

What kind of place are
you looking for?

(*Still without volume,
an advertisement for
Miracle Headache Pills:
a woman is seen before
and after taking the
pills.*)

HAL

I'd like to find an apartment with more than one
small room for under a
hundred dollars.

SUSAN

Do you want to live in the
Village?

HAL
Makes no difference.

GEORGE
Don't live down there.

SUSAN
Why not?

GEORGE
It's too crowded.

SUSAN
It's not so crowded, and
in the Village you can see
a lot of wonderful faces.

GEORGE
Yes, well frankly I've been
working for a living for
twenty-one years and I re-
sent having to support a
lot of bums on relief.

SUSAN
That's not the Village.
That's the Bowery.

*(Lady Announcer be-
gins to speak, still without volume.)*

GEORGE
Let's not talk about it.

SUSAN
Why not?

*(Slide: First Federal
Savings Bank.)*

GEORGE

I already told Hal that people with differing points of view shouldn't talk about politics. And I shouldn't be eating this cake either.

(*snaps volume on*)

LADY ANNOUNCER

And now First Federal Savings and Kennel-Heart Dog Food present Luncheon With Carol, a program especially designed for the up-to-date woman. Our topic for today: I Quit. And here's Carol.

(*Slide: Carol and Ron Campbell.*)

CAROL

Hello, ladies. This is Carol. I have as my guest today Mr. Ron Campbell just back from an eighteen month tour of duty in Vietnam. Mr. Campbell was a member of the famed Green Berets. He is a holder of the Bronze Star and the South Vietnamese Order of Merit; he has been nominated for the U.S. Silver Star. A few weeks ago he was offered a field commission as captain. But instead of accepting, what did you do, Ron?

RON
I quit.

CAROL
That's right, you quit.
Tell us why you quit,
Ron, when you were ob-
viously doing so well.

RON
I didn't like being there.

CAROL
You didn't?

RON
No.

CAROL (*cheerfully*)
I see.

RON
We're committing mass
murder.

CAROL (*interested*)
Yes?

RON
We're trying to take over
a people that don't want
to be taken over by any-
body.

CAROL
Now, Ron, American boys are out there dying so somebody must be doing something wrong somewhere.

RON
Whoever in Hanoi or Peking or Washington is sending men out to be killed, THEY'RE doing something wrong.

CAROL (*interested in his opinion, tolerant*)
I see.

RON
You do? Well I was there for a year and a half and every day I saw things that would make you sick. Heads broken, babies smashed against walls—

CAROL (*deeply sympathetic*)
I KNOW.

RON
You know?

CAROL
War is horrible.

RON
> Listen—

CAROL
> Thank you, Ron. We've
> been talking this after-
> noon, ladies, with Ron
> Campbell, war hero.

RON
> Will you let me say some-
> thing, please?

CAROL (*tolerating   him,
>   kindly*)
> And a fascinating talk it's
> been, Ron, but I'm afraid
> our time is up.

RON
> One—

CAROL (*with her special
>   smile for the ladies*)
> Ladies, see you all tomor-
> row.

SUSAN (*dreamily*)
> I think I'm floating fur-
> ther and further left.

GEORGE
> You don't know a thing
> about it.

SUSAN
I was listening to Norman
Thomas last night—

LADY ANNOUNCER
This program was brought
to you by First Federal
Savings and Kennel-Heart
Dog Food. The opinions
expressed on this program
are not necessarily those
of anyone connected with
it. A dog in the home
means a dog with a heart.

(*Slide: Kennel-Heart
Dog Food.*)

GEORGE
I'm going to the Men's
Room.

LADY ANNOUNCER
Kennel-Heart.   Bow-wow.
Wow.

SUSAN
Poor George.

(*Slide: "Billion Dollar
Movie."*)

HAL
You still haven't told me
about tonight.

SUSAN
Told you what about to-
night?

(*A very English man
and a very English
woman appear in the
movie.*)

HE
Sarah.

SHE
Yes, Richard.

HAL
Are we going to the movies or are we not going to the movies?

HE
Our old apartment.

SUSAN
I don't know. I can't make up my mind.

SHE
Yes, Richard. It's still here.

HAL
That's just fine.

HE
It seems very small to me.

SHE
It does to me, too.

SUSAN
I want to work on my apartment.

HAL
Okay.

HE
Do you think we can live in it again?

SHE
Not in the old way.

SUSAN
I should really get it done.

HE
> In a better way.

HAL
> You're right.

SHE
> You've changed too, Richard, for the better.

HE
> So have you, darling, for the better.

SUSAN
> Suppose I let you know by the end of the afternoon?

HAL
> Suppose we forget I ever suggested it.

SHE
> I've learned a lot.

HE
> Maybe that's what war is for.

> (*The People On Television hum "White Cliffs of Dover" under the following.*)

SHE
> The brick wall in front of the window is gone.

HE
We'll rebuild for the future.

SUSAN
Oh, all right, I'll go.
Happy?

HAL
I'm so happy I could put
a bullet through my brain.

SHE
I hope there is never any
more war. Ever, ever
again.

HE
Amen.

(*Slide: "The End."*)

(*The People On Television sing, meaningfully, the last line of
"White Cliffs of Dover": "Tomorrow, just you wait and see."*)

SUSAN
Sugar?

HAL
You're like my grandmother.

(*First News Announcer
appears.*)

SUSAN
How?

HAL
She asked me if I took sugar every day we lived together. It was very comforting.

(*Slide: baseball player.*)

FIRST NEWS ANNOUNCER
Baseball's Greg Pironelli, fifty-six, died today of a heart attack in St. Petersburg, Florida. He hit a total of four hundred and eighty home runs and had a lifetime batting average of three forty-one.

HAL
Hal, she used to say to me, my grandmother, you're going to be a big man.

(*Slide: a baseball game.*)

HAL
Everybody's going to love you. She used to sing that song to me: "Poppa's gonna buy you a dog named Rover, and if that dog don't bark, Poppa's gonna buy you a looking glass, and if that looking glass should break, you're still the sweetest little boy in town."

FIRST NEWS ANNOUNCER
In 1963, the year he was elected to baseball's hall of fame in Cooperstown, New York, Pironelli suffered his first stroke. Pironelli owned a Florida-wide chain of laundries.

(*Slide: "Johnny Holland Show."*)

JOHNNY
We're back.

> (*Slide: Johnny and Luci.*)

JOHNNY
That's a very pretty dress you've got on, Luci.

SUSAN
That's nice.

LUCI
Thank you, Johnny.

> (*George enters and goes directly to telephone.*)

GEORGE
Hello, darling? Listen, I've gotten out of it. Isn't that good news? The midnight shift.

JOHNNY
How does it feel living in Austin after all the excitement of the big wedding?

LUCI
It feels fine.

GEORGE
I'm looking forward to being home nice and comfy with you.

JOHNNY
Do you miss your father?

GEORGE
You know my stomach is killing me. Sure I will. Wait a minute.

LUCI
Oh sure, I miss him.

(*George takes out a pencil.*)

GEORGE

Toothpaste. Cauliflower. That's a good idea.

JOHNNY (*awkward pause*)

I guess your heart belongs to Daddy, huh?

GEORGE

Large face cream. Why large? No, I don't care. I was just asking.

LUCI

That's right.

JOHNNY (*awkward pause*)

Is your father hard to get along with?

GEORGE

Okay. Listen, I'm really looking forward to seeing you.

LUCI

Oh, no. When I want something I just march right in, cuddle up in his lap, and give him a great big kiss.

(*Slide: a second view of Johnny and Luci.*)

JOHNNY (*awkward pause*)

So you'd say your father is affectionate?

LUCI
Very affectionate.

GEORGE
No, I haven't been drink-
ing, and it's rotten of you
to ask.

JOHNNY (*awkward pause*)
Does he ever ask your ad-
vice about important mat-
ters?

GEORGE
Okay, okay. Bye.
(*hangs up telephone*)

LUCI
Well, one day I told him
what I thought, good and
proper, about all those
nervous nellies interfering
with my Daddy's war.

(*Johnny does a double
take of scandalized
amusement to the au-
dience.*)

(*Slide: Johnny doing
double take.*)

JOHNNY
And what did he say?

LUCI
He laughed.

SUSAN
Have a little coffee,
George.

GEORGE
No, thanks.

HAL
Oh, come on, George,
have a little coffee.

GEORGE
A sip.

JOHNNY
It's lovely talking to you,
Luci.

SUSAN
Sugar or superine?

LUCI
It's nice talking to you
too, Johnny.

GEORGE
Sugar.

JOHNNY
We'll be back.

SUSAN
George.

(*Slide: "Johnny Holland Show."*)

GEORGE
Don't take care of me. I
said sugar.

SUSAN
Whatever   you   want,
George.

(*An Evangelist appears
with his choir, which is
singing "Onward Chris-
tian Soldiers."*)

(*Slide: the Evangelist.*)

EVANGELIST
If we could look through
the ceiling of this wonderful new air-conditioned
stadium we could see the
stars. Nonetheless I have
heard them in faraway
countries, I have heard
them criticize, criticize us
and the leaders we know
and love.

SUSAN
George, what are you eat-
ing now?

GEORGE
Chicken sandwich.

SUSAN
Give me a bite.

(*Hal plays with his pen-
knife. Susan eats an-
other piece of cake.
George eats his chicken
sandwich.*)

EVANGELIST
Why? Well I will tell you
why. They criticize us because we are rich, as if
money itself were evil.
Money, the Bible says, is
the root of evil, not evil
itself. I have seen a room-

ful of men and women, powerful Hollywood celebrities at four o'clock A.M. in the morning, listening to me with tears streaming down their faces crying out to me that they had lost touch with God.

(*George starts to cough.*)

EVANGELIST
"In God We Trust" is on our coins, ladies and gentlemen—

(*Slide: a second view of the Evangelist.*)

SUSAN
What's the matter, George?

(*The evangelist choir sings "Onward Christian Soldiers."*)

(*George motions her away and continues to cough.*)

HAL (*turning volume off*)   (*Volume off.*)
Spit it out, George.

SUSAN
Hal, leave him alone.

HAL

George, spit it out.
(*thumps George on the
back*)

SUSAN

Hal! George, is it epi-
lepsy?

HAL

It's something in his
throat.

SUSAN

Try to tell us what it is,
George.

HAL AND GEORGE

Chicken!

HAL

He has a chicken bone
stuck in his throat.

SUSAN

Oh my God. Well give
him some water.

(*George's choking is
getting worse.*)

HAL

Water will wash right by
it. Let me look.

(*holds George's head and looks into his mouth*)
Don't move, George. I want to take a look.
(*looks in George's mouth*)
There it is.

SUSAN (*also looking*)
Ugh, it's stuck in his throat. I'll get some water.

(*Hal and Susan let go of George, who falls to the floor.*)

HAL
Not water.

SUSAN
Why not?

HAL
Because water will wash right past the thing. It needs something to push it out.

SUSAN
Like what?

HAL

Like bread.

SUSAN

Bread? Bread will get
stuck on the bone and
he'll choke.

HAL

You're wrong.

SUSAN

I'm right.

HAL

Bread will push it right
down.

SUSAN

Water will do that.

HAL

You're wrong.

SUSAN

It's you that's wrong and
won't admit it.

HAL

I'm going to give him
some bread.

SUSAN

I won't allow it.

HAL

    YOU won't allow it?

SUSAN

    It'll kill him.

HAL

    He's choking right now
    and I'm going to give him
    some of this bread.

SUSAN

    Give him water.

HAL

    I said bread.

SUSAN (*starting to walk past*
    Hal)
    And I said water.

HAL (*grabbing her arm*)
    Bread.

SUSAN

    Water. Ow, you're hurt-
    ing me.

      (*George is having a*
      very bad time. Hal and
      Susan turn to look at
      him, speaking softly.)

SUSAN
   Let's call the operator.

HAL
   It would take too long.

SUSAN
   And he wouldn't like anyone to see him.

HAL
   Why not?

SUSAN
   I don't know.

   (At this point George
   finally coughs the thing
   up, and his cough sub-
   sides into an animal
   pant.)

SUSAN (going to him, pat-
     ting him)
   Poor George.

HAL
   It's over.

SUSAN
   No thanks to you.

HAL
  Nor you.

SUSAN (*putting George's
    head on her breast*)
He might have choked.
Poor George.

GEORGE (*pushing her away*)
Fuck!

> (*George lurches against
> the console on his way
> to the bathroom, acci-
> dentally turning on the
> volume.*)

EVANGELIST   CHOIR   (*still
    singing "Onward Chris-
    tian Soldiers."*)
"With the cross of
Jesus—"

> (*Hal changes channels
> from the Evangelist's
> meeting to "My Favor-
> ite Teenager."*)

> (*Slide: Mother, Father,
> and Daughter in "My
> Favorite Teenager."*)

SUSAN (*sitting in her chair*)
Poor George.

MOTHER
  Why aren't you going?

DAUGHTER   (*sitting   in
    George's chair at the
    control console*)

Because I told Harold
Sternpepper he could take
me.

MOTHER
Yes, and—

DAUGHTER
Well, Harold Sternpepper
is a creep. Everybody
knows that.

(*The remaining People
On Television make the
sound of canned laugh-
ter.*)

HAL (*sitting in his chair*)
What movie are we going
to?

MOTHER
So, why—

DAUGHTER
Oh, because I was mad at
Gail.

(*Canned laughter.*)

SUSAN
I don't know.

MOTHER
What about Johnny Beau-
mont?

HAL
What about George?

SUSAN
What about him?

DAUGHTER
What about him?

HAL
Well, I guess it's none of
my business.

MOTHER
Well, I guess it's none of
my business.

GEORGE (*returning*)
What's the matter?

FATHER
What's the matter?

(*Slide: second view of
Mother, Father, and
Daughter in "My Fa-
vorite Teenager."*)

SUSAN
Nothing.

DAUGHTER
Nothing.

GEORGE
Going somewhere?

FATHER
Why aren't you dressed
for the prom?

DAUGHTER
I'm not going to the
prom.

SUSAN
We're going to the mov-
ies.

FATHER
Why not? Why isn't she
going, Grace?

(*Hal and Susan and George are slowing down because they are mesmerized by "My Favorite Teenager."*)

GEORGE
What movie are you going to?

GEORGE
Mind if I come along?

SUSAN
Oh, George, you don't really want to.

GEORGE
I'd be pleased as punch.

MOTHER
Don't ask me. I just live here.

(*Canned laughter.*)

FATHER
Why doesn't anybody tell me anything around here?

(*Canned laughter.*)

DAUGHTER (*getting up from George's chair*)
Oh, why don't you two leave me alone? I'm not going because nobody's taking me.

FATHER (*sitting in George's chair*)
Nobody's taking my little girl to the junior prom? I'll take her myself.

DAUGHTER (*stifling a yelp of horror*)
Oh no, Daddy, don't bother. I mean how would it look, I mean—

FATHER
I'd be pleased as punch.

SUSAN
Hal, say something.

HAL (*to George*)
You look bushed to me,
George.

GEORGE
Who's bushed?

(*George sits in his
chair.*)

(*Hal, Susan, and
George are completely
mesmerized by the TV
show.*)

DAUGHTER (*aside to Mother*)
Help.

(*Canned laughter.*)

MOTHER (*to Father*)
Now, dear, don't you
think for your age—

(*Canned laughter.*)

FATHER
My age?

(*Canned laughter.*)

FATHER (*standing and doing
a two-step*)
I'd like to see anybody
laugh at my two-step.

(*Canned laughter.*)

DAUGHTER (*in despair*)
Oh, Daddy. Mother, DO
something.

(*Canned laughter.*)

MOTHER (*putting her arm
around George's shoul-
ders*)

I think it's a very nice
idea. And maybe I'll go
with Harold Sternpepper.

(*Canned laughter.*)

DAUGHTER (*loudly, sitting on
Hal's knee*)
Oh, Mother, oh, Daddy,
oh no!

(*The canned laughter
mounts. Music.*)

(*Slide: "My Favorite
Teenager."*)

(*Now they all speak like situation-comedy characters.*)

HAL
What movie shall we go
to?

GEORGE
Let's talk about it over
dinner.

HAL
Who said anything about
dinner?

(*All of the People On
Television do canned
laughter now. They are
crowded around the
control console.*)

SUSAN

Isn't anybody going to ask
me what I want to do?

(*Canned laughter.*)

GEORGE

Sure, what do you want,
Susan?

HAL

It's up to you.

(*Slide: Hal, Susan, and
George with the same
facial expressions they
now have on the stage.*)

SUSAN

Well, have I got a surprise
for you two. I'M going
home to fix up my apart-
ment and you two can
have dinner TOGETHER.

(*Hal, Susan, and George join in the canned laughter.
Then, lights off. Slide off. Curtain call: all are in the
same position, silent, their faces frozen into laughing
masks.*)

MOTEL

A Masque for Three Dolls

... after all our subtle colour and nervous rhythm, after the faint mixed tints of Conder, what more is possible? After us the Savage God.

W.B. Yeats

MOTEL (under the title AMERICA HURRAH) was first presented at the Cafe La Mama, in the spring of 1965, directed by Michael Kahn.

The actors in the dolls in the 1966 Pocket Theatre production:

Motel-Keeper	Brenda Smiley
Man	Conard Fowkes
Woman	James Barbosa

Motel-Keeper's Voice: Ruth White

Music: Marianne de Pury

Lights come up on the Motel-Keeper doll. The intensity of the light will increase as the play continues.

The Motel-Keeper doll is large, much larger than human size, but the impression of hugeness can come mainly from the fact that her head is at least three times larger than would be normal in proportion to her body. She is all gray. She has a large full skirt which reaches to the floor. She has squarish breasts. The hair curlers on her head suggest electronic receivers.

The Motel-Keeper doll has eyeglasses which are mirrors. It doesn't matter what these mirrors reflect at any given moment. The audience may occasionally catch a glimpse of itself, or be bothered by reflections of light in the mirrors. It doesn't matter; the sensory nerves of the audience are not to be spared.

The motel room in which the Motel-Keeper doll stands is anonymously modern, except for certain "homey" touches. A neon light blinks outside the window. The colors in the room, like the colors in the clothes on the Man and Woman dolls, are violent combinations of oranges, pinks, and reds against a reflective plastic background.

The Motel-Keeper's Voice, which never stops, comes from a loudspeaker, or from several loudspeakers in the theatre. The Voice will be, at first, mellow and husky and then, as the light grows harsher and brighter, the Voice will grow harsher too, more set in its pattern, hard finally, and patronizing and petty.

An actor on platform shoes works the Motel-Keeper doll from inside it. The actor can move only the doll's arms or its entire body. As the Voice begins, the arms move, and then the Motel-Keeper doll fusses about the room in little circles.

MOTEL-KEEPER'S VOICE.   I am old. I am an old idea: the walls; that from which it springs forth. I enclose the nothing, making then a place in which it happens. I am the room: a Roman theatre where cheers break loose the lion; a railroad carriage in the forest at Compiègne, in 1918, and in 1941. I have been rooms of marble and rooms of cork, all letting forth an avalanche. Rooms of mud and rooms of silk. This room will be slashed too, as if by a scimitar, its contents spewed and yawned out. That is what happens. It is almost happening, in fact. I am this room.

(*As the Motel-Keeper's Voice continues, the doors at the back of the room open and headlights shine into the eyes of the audience; passing in front of the headlights, in silhouette, we see two more huge dolls, the Man and the Woman.*)

MOTEL-KEEPER'S VOICE. It's nice; not so fancy as some, but with all the conveniences. And a touch of home. The antimacassar comes from my mother's house in Boise. Boise, Idaho. Sits kind of nice, I think, on the Swedish swing. That's my own idea, you know. All modern, up-to-date, that's it—no motel on this route is more up-to-date. Or cleaner. Go look, then talk me a thing or two.

(*The Woman doll enters. Her shoulders are thrown way back, like a girl posing for a calendar. Her breasts are particularly large and perfect, wiggleable if possible. She has a cherry-lipstick smile, blond hair, and a garish patterned dress.*

Both the Man and the Woman dolls are the same size as the Motel-Keeper doll, with heads at least three times larger than would be normal for their bodies. The Man and the Woman dolls, however, are flesh-colored and have more mobility. The actors inside these dolls are also on platform shoes. There is absolutely no rapport between the Motel-Keeper and the Man and Woman. All of the Motel-Keeper's remarks are addressed generally. She is never directly motivated by the actions of the Man and Woman dolls.

As the Woman doll enters, she puts down her purse and inspects the room. Then she takes off her dress, revealing lace panties and bra.)

MOTEL-KEEPER'S VOICE.   All modern here but, as I say, with the tang of home. Do you understand? When folks are fatigued, in a strange place? Not that it's old-fashioned. No. Not in the wrong way. There's a push-button here for TV. The toilet flushes of its own accord. All you've got to do is get off. Pardon my mentioning it, but you'll have to go far before you see a thing like that on this route. Oh, it's quite a room. Yes. And reasonable. Sign here. Pardon the pen leak. I can see you're fatigued.

(The Woman doll goes into the bathroom.)

MOTEL-KEEPER'S VOICE.   Any children? Well, that's nice. Children don't appreciate travel. And rooms don't appreciate children. As it happens it's the last one I've got left. I'll just flip my vacancy switch. Twelve dollars, please. In advance that'll be. That way you can go any time you want to go, you know, get an early start. On a trip to see sights, are you? That's nice. You just get your luggage while I unlock the room. You can see the light.

(The Man doll enters carrying a suitcase. He has a cigar and a loud Florida shirt. He closes the door, inspects the

room, and takes off his clothes, except for his loudly pat-
terned shorts.)

MOTEL-KEEPER'S VOICE.   There now. What I say doesn't matter. You can see. It speaks for itself. The room speaks for
itself. You can see it's a perfect 1966 room. But a taste of
home. I've seen to that. A taste of home.
Comfy, cozy, nice, but a taste of newness. That's what.
You can see it.
The best stop on route Six Sixty-Six. Well, there might be
others like it, but this is the best stop. You've arrived at the
right place. This place. And a hooked rug. I don't care
what, but I've said no room IS without a hooked rug.

(Sound of the toilet flushing.)

MOTEL-KEEPER'S VOICE.   No complaints yet. Never. Modern
people like modern places. Oh yes. I can tell. They tell me.
And reasonable. Very very reasonable rates. No cheaper
rates on the route, not for this. You receive what you pay
for.

(Sound of the toilet flushing again.)

MOTEL-KEEPER'S VOICE.   All that driving and driving and driving. Fatigued. You must be. I would be. Miles and miles
and miles.

*(The Man doll begins an inspection of the bed. He pulls
at the bedspread, testing its strength.)*

MOTEL-KEEPER'S VOICE.   Fancy. Fancy your ending up right
here. You didn't know and I didn't know. But you did. End

up right here. Respectable and decent and homelike. Right here.

(*The Woman doll comes back from the bathroom to get her negligee from her purse. She returns to the bathroom.*)

MOTEL-KEEPER'S VOICE. All folks everywhere sitting in the very palm of God. Waiting, whither, whence.

(*The Man doll pulls the bedspread, blankets, and sheets off the bed, tearing them apart. He jumps hard on the bed.*)

MOTEL-KEEPER'S VOICE. Any motel you might have come to on Six Sixty-Six. Any motel. On that vast network of roads Whizzing by, whizzing by. Trucks too. And cars from everywhere. Full up with folks, all sitting in the very palm of God. I can tell proper folks when I get a look at them. All folks.

(*The Man doll rummages through the suitcase, throwing clothes about the room.*)

MOTEL-KEEPER'S VOICE. Country roads, state roads, United States roads. It's a big world and here you are. I noticed you got a license plate. I've not been to there myself. I've not been to anywhere myself, excepting town for supplies, and Boise. Boise, Idaho.

(*Toilet articles and bathroom fixtures, including toilet paper and the toilet seat, are thrown out of the bath-*

room. The Man doll casually tears pages out of the Bible.)

MOTEL-KEEPER'S VOICE. The world arrives to me, you'd say. It's a small world. These plastic flowers here: "Made in Japan" on the label. You noticed? Got them from the catalogue. Cat-al-ogue. Every product in this room is ordered.

(The Man doll pulls down some of the curtains. Objects continue to be thrown from the bathroom.)

MOTEL-KEEPER'S VOICE. Ordered from the catalogue. Excepting the antimacassars and the hooked rug. Made the hooked rug myself. Tang of home. No room is a room without. Course the bedspread, hand-hooked, hooked near here at town. Mrs. Harritt. Betsy Harritt gets materials through another catalogue. Cat-al-ogue.

(The Woman doll comes out of the bathroom wearing her negligee over her panties and bra. When the Man doll notices her, he stops his other activities and goes to her.)

MOTEL-KEEPER'S VOICE. Myself, I know it from the catalogue: bottles, bras, breakfasts, refrigerators, cast iron gates, plastic posies,

(The Woman doll opens her negligee and the Man doll pulls off her bra. The Man and Woman dolls embrace. The Woman doll puts lipstick on her nipples.)

MOTEL-KEEPER'S VOICE. paper subscriptions, Buick trucks, blankets, forks, clitter-clack darning hooks, transistors and antimacassar, vinyl plastics,

(*The Man doll turns on the TV. It glares viciously and plays loud rock and roll music.*)

MOTEL-KEEPER'S VOICE.   crazy quilts, paper hairpins, cats, catnip, club feet, canisters, banisters, holy books, tattooed toilet articles, tables, tea cozies,

(*The Man doll writes simple obscene words on the wall. The Woman doll does the same with her lipstick.*)

MOTEL-KEEPER'S VOICE.   pickles, bayberry candles, South Dakotan Kewpie Dolls, fiberglass hair, polished milk, amiable grandpappies, colts, Galsworthy books, cribs, cabinets, teeter-totters,

(*The Woman doll has turned to picture-making. She draws a crude cock and coyly adds pubic hair and drops of come.*)

MOTEL-KEEPER'S VOICE.   and television sets.
Oh I tell you it, I do. It's a wonder. Full with things, the world, full up. Shall I tell you my thought? Next year there's a shelter to be built by me, yes. Shelter motel. Everything to be placed under the ground. Signs up in every direction up and down Six Sixty-Six.

(*The Man and Woman dolls twist.*)

MOTEL-KEEPER'S VOICE.   Complete Security, Security While You Sleep Tight, Bury Your Troubles At This Motel, Homelike, Very Comfy, and Encased In Lead, Every Room Its Own Set, Fourteen Day Emergency Supplies $5.00 Extra,

(*The rock and roll music gets louder and louder. A civil-defense siren, one long wail, begins to build. The Man*